MW01241912

DO YOU MIND
IF WE HAVE SEX
IN THE
BACKSEAT?

Susan W Shafer

DO YOU MIND IF WE HAVE SEX IN THE BACKSEAT?

Susan W Shafer

(Formerly Corbran)

Other books by Susan W Corbran (Shafer)
Sam and the Mysterious Blue Car, E-book and paperback, 2019
You'll Always Be Close to My Heart, E-book and paperback, 2017
5 Simple Ways to Love Gay Christians, E-book, 2017

Do You Mind If We Have Sex in the Backseat?

Copyright © 2019 by Susan W Shafer

All rights reserved. No part of this book may be reproduced in any form or by any electronic or mechanical means including information storage and retrieval systems, without permission in writing from the author. The only exception is by a reviewer, who may quote short excerpts in a review.

Cover and Interior designed by Susan W Shafer
This book is a work of non-fiction. No passenger names are listed. Names of places, restaurants, cities are in the vicinity of Charlotte, NC.

Susan W Shafer (formerly Corbran)
@swshafertheauthor (Facebook)

First Printing: November 2019

ISBN-13 978-1-078443173

Printed in the United States of America

"Do You Mind If We Have Sex in the Backseat?" is dedicated to the 5000 plus people who have ridden in my car since August 2016.

* * *

Thanks for sharing your stories, jobs, family, and activities. Without you, this book would be impossible to write.

CONTENTS

Preface

There's a coverless road atlas with tears in the pages in the trunk of my car. I used it for many road trips across the eastern states. When I came upon cars backed up on the highway, I could look at my trusty map to find a road off the beaten path. It was on that road where I would discover amazing places.

Nowadays, I rely on Google Maps to take me from point A to point B. Although a road map is handy in the daytime, it's almost impossible to use it at night. Having a lighted map on my phone attached to the air vent is the next best thing.

No matter what method we use, a person knowing their destination will always be the way to go, except if they are sleeping. Then it's up to us.

Our destinations often change from day to day, We add stops along the way, and sometimes we need to make a U-turn to go back for a forgotten item. However long it takes, we'll eventually arrive at our intended destination.

* * *

After driving for several months in Charlotte, I realized this was a "meant for me" job. I had been primed by driving my six kids to school, jobs, sports, or to see friends, and then back home. I was doing this for over ten years without compensation.

My love for driving was passed down from my parents. They enjoyed day trips around the county, traveling on back roads, while I sat in the backseat watching the houses and trees fly by.

Every experience in our past has been for a steppingstone toward the future. Our paths often crisscross, but eventually, we'll arrive at the next destination.

✳ ✳ ✳

People ask, "What's it about being a driver that you love the most?"

"I love having the flexibility to choose when and how long to drive. Although I'm not a morning person, there have been days when I've woken early to drive a friend to the airport. Plus, I can work around doctor appointments and road trips to visit grandkids."

✳ ✳ ✳

As you glance through the pages, you will notice that each chapter is a letter in the alphabet. Such as, Chapter 14 is the letter N stands for Nauseated Episodes. Are you curious if anyone has ever thrown up in my car?

And if you wondered if someone had sex in the backseat, you'll find that answer in Chapter 19, Sex, Drugs, But No Tricks.

This book makes a great gift for those who love to read, travel, or is simply curious. When you've finished reading, please leave a review on Amazon. Thank you.

CHAPTER 1 – AWAY WE GO

There is a designated parking lot for rideshare drivers. When you enter the queue, you are given the number of drivers ahead of you. The longest I've had to wait was two hours, and the shortest was a matter of seconds – sometimes getting pinged before I even entered the lot.

The advantage of bringing a passenger to the airport is the likelihood that you're going to get a ride to leave the airport. After dropping the passenger off at the departure area, I take the time to call the next passenger and tell them I must drive around the loop to then return to the arrival area of the terminal. I inquire about what color shirt or jacket they're wearing, so I can find them easier. If I get to the pickup zone and they're not ready, the security attendants might send me back around the loop, which costs more money for longer wait times. Plus, the chance of having the ride canceled.

One afternoon, I picked up a woman at the airport who came to visit her daughter and granddaughter, as it was a few months since she'd seen them. We enjoyed a pleasant conversation during the 38-minute drive to her house. Before arriving, the woman questioned whether she would be able to get into the house. I told her I would wait in the driveway to make sure. The woman looked under the doormat but didn't find a key. Not only was she locked out, but there was no chair or bench to sit down and wait unless she wanted to sit on the sidewalk.

As a driver, I felt bad about leaving her sitting on a suitcase at the front door, so I offered to drive to her daughter's workplace, which was another ten-minutes away. After arriving, the woman called to get the car keys so she could wait in the car, but the daughter was too busy. So, for the next thirty minutes, I sat in my car with this woman (and her luggage) waiting patiently for her daughter to come outside. By this time, I finished the ride and went offline, so no one else could ask for a ride. When she finally walked out, she decided she would go home too. The woman thanked me several times and waved as I drove away.

✳ ✳ ✳

Sitting in the queue can be frustrating, especially when you accidentally fall asleep and miss a ride. When I woke up and realized I didn't have time to accept it, they put me at the end of the line. Since I had already waited more than thirty minutes, I left the lot. Sometimes I stay depending on how many drivers are ahead.

One evening, I finally got to the "next in line" in the queue. I put my seatbelt on, ready to start the car at a moment's notice. I waited for 40 minutes, and I was still in the queue. I understood the problem. Sometimes drivers get short rides, and then the app promises them first or second in line when they get back to the lot. By then, I was tired of waiting, and so I turned the app off and went home. If I chose to stay after getting a short ride, the following one would be longer.

✳ ✳ ✳

There's never a good time to go through a red light. I was making sure you were paying attention. You can, however, stop and then turn right if there's not a "No turn on red" sign.

One day as I was leaving the terminal with a passenger, I glanced at my GPS to see if I should go to the right, straight, or left at the first major intersection. At that moment, I saw the map highlighted for me to go to the second intersection and turn left onto the interstate. I got in the straight lane but was next to the left turn only lane. When I glanced at the map again, I realized I was supposed to turn left on that road.

Being first in line, I decided that maybe if I went fast enough, I could go ahead of the car beside me while turning left. When the light turned green, I tried, but to no avail, there was only one way to go, and that was straight. Someone on the other side was honking their horn. I was like, "What's your problem?!" and then realized I had gone through a red light. "Oops."

✻ ✻ ✻

A young man had a connecting flight from Charlotte canceled because it was going to be on a 737 plane, the same kind that had crashed overseas twice that spring. Many of the planes were grounded across the country, changing thousands of flights.

Since his next flight wasn't until the following day, I told him about the ACC Basketball games and other activities he might take advantage of while he was in town. He was fortunate to have a friend close by to offer him a couch to sleep.

✻ ✻ ✻

A young man in his mid-20s had returned home from a nine-day trip to Colombia, South America. He met a young woman online and chatted online, even for six hours at a time. After several months, they decided it was time to meet in person.

Curious about that country, I asked him if there were soldiers in view, and he said yes. His mom told him to locate the US Embassy when he arrived and to be very careful when out and about the cities there. He said the Embassy was 19 hours away. He added that there were US Coast Guards outside his window. (or at the complex he was in).

He showed me a picture of his girlfriend. I agreed she was cute. He told me that she's teaching him Spanish and that she wants to come to the US and become a nanny. I told him about Charlotte's Best Nanny (my friends own the company). Unfortunately, neither of us had anything to write that down on, and he left thinking that I forgot to text it to him, but I tried but was no longer able to through the rideshare app.

Anyway - while he was there, he bought jewelry for the girl and, he had presents for his family. It was an interesting ride.

* * *

After dropping a man off at his destination, he asked if I would pick him back up at 4 pm and take him to the airport. I did it on my own time. I charged him $15, and he gave me $30. Sweet deal.

* * *

Not being a drinker myself, it's hard to recommend a favorite hangout in Charlotte except for knowing where I drop other passengers off. One young man, who had a layover, wanted to go to a popular bar. It took me a while to remember where some of these places were, though I knew I was in the general area. I felt like I was driving in circles. Finally, I pulled in front of a pizza and beer joint that offered outside seating and large TVs to watch sports or the news. (After driving for three years, I have a better understanding of where to find the popular craft beer joints.)

* * *

The employees at the airport also use the rideshare app. Most live close to work, which means it doesn't provide the driver with much money. Some drivers refuse to pick them up. It doesn't bother me as I take every opportunity to meet people, gaining one story at a time.

* * *

A mom was soon to be surprised to discover her children coming into the front of her home within hours of each other. She had no idea this was taking place since she had made other plans and had invited out of town guests in for a holiday.

The young man I picked up at the airport had to call those guests and cancel their trip. He shared the surprise with them so they wouldn't share it with their mom. Thankfully, the dad was in on the surprise.

I suggest him to videotape his mom's response, so maybe it would go viral.

Although the siblings knew the other guests, they wanted to spend the holiday with their immediate family.

Though when the young man found out that his brother wasn't coming the night as previously thought. He was like - 'who am I going to go drinking with tonight?' I guess he spent the evening with his parents instead.

CHAPTER 2– BLIND AND DEAF

After pulling my car alongside a driveway, I noticed two boys playing in the yard and a woman walking toward the car. The boys stopped what they were doing and came over to the car. After opening the back door, they climbed in but forgot to close the door. As the woman approached the car, I saw she was reaching for the front seat door, so I reminded her to close the back door.

It was then that I noticed that she was visually impaired. I asked with permission what age she was when she lost her sight. She said since birth. She admitted she has both a walking cane and a service dog but felt confident to leave them home that day. I dropped them off at a restaurant near the front door. Her boys helped by opening the other door for her. She walked in without any other help.

I drove into my old apartment complex and saw two people waiting near the entrance, but only one got into the car. I turned the car around and told the woman that I used to live there. But she looked confused. I thought perhaps she didn't speak English, so I tried to use hand motions that would tell her that I slept in the building. She finally pointed to her ears, and I realized that she couldn't hear me. The rest of the ride was very quiet.

Several times I've had to fold wheelchairs or strollers and put them in the trunk. When you don't do it often, it's easy to forget how simple it can be.

✴ ✴ ✴

I got a ping to pick up a man at an apartment complex. He called me to say where he would be standing. I pulled in, and there was a van parked near the curb. I looked and saw him standing near the front of the van. After a few minutes, I saw his walking cane and figured he was visually impaired. He said that he could see shadows but not definite colors.

His destination was the library to vote. After dropping him off and helping him get to the door, I noticed there was no line. I parked the car and went in to vote. I was going to suggest to him that I'd wait and then drive him back but then saw another worker reading everything to him and decided it was going to take a while, so I left.

✴ ✴ ✴

I arrived at the shopping plaza and looked around to find my passenger. I saw a young man holding a guide stick as well as his phone and decided he was my passenger. I was right. He called, and I told him I was nearby and pulled up beside him. He said he could see shadows. He holds a full-time job and listens to music in his spare time.

CHAPTER 3 – COLLISIONS

There are days when you can't take your eyes off the road. The traffic in and around Charlotte can be a bear. Thankfully, it's not too often when I need to pump the brakes to keep cars from hitting me. The crazier episodes are when some idiots (and I don't say that lightly) race through the traffic, to the right, and then to the left, to get ahead of the pack. It's downright scary at times. It makes you wonder if you're in the middle of filming an action movie.

✳ ✳ ✳

One night as I pulled up to a red traffic light, I noticed a car sitting in the middle of the road facing in the opposite direction with its lights on. The front of the car was against the median. The driver was leaning on the steering wheel with his head down. I honked several times, but there was no movement.

Then another car pulled up to the light, and I motioned to them to notice the car. As the young man got out of his car, I pulled my car over to the side of the road and put the hazard lights on. I followed him to the car in question. The young man knocked on the window until the driver sat up. He asked him to put the car in park, but instead, the driver took off down the road.

A police car happened to come up to the intersection, and we told her what happened, and she did a quick U-turn and went after the car.

Sharing the story with friends, they remind me how dangerous that could have ended – for both the young man and me. Doing a good deed isn't as simple as it used to be. Keeping an eye on the surroundings is smarter.

* * *

I picked up a young man in a wheelchair. He sat in the front seat, which was nice so that we could have a conversation. I put his chair in the trunk. His destination took south on I-77. As I drove passed exit 9, two cars whizzed past. I told him, "There goes an accident waiting to happen." Within minutes, we saw a cloud of black smoke. Cars in front of us were slowing down; some were stopping. I inched my way into the midst of the smoke. A black sedan had spun out of control and went backward into a cement barrier. The second car was seen zooming backward on the side of the road, perhaps going to see if the other driver was okay.

I glanced over at the black car. The driver was coherent and alert, so I kept driving. Other stopped cars were starting to move. Suddenly, I saw the black car in my rearview mirror. It was directly behind me. I watched it slowly move around me and pass me on the right. I noticed the license plate and memorized it for my safety. No sooner did I watch it go by, when the second car, a smaller red sedan drove past on my left. As soon as it was two car lengths ahead, I heard what sounded like firecrackers.

My passenger shouted, "Who's he shooting at?"

The thought of it being gunfire made the event worse. All I wanted to do was to drop my passenger off and go home. The next exit was his. I pulled off the road and drove up the ramp. The two cars were parked, one in front of the other, and the drivers were standing outside facing each other. I quickly looked at the red car's license plate, but it was a temporary one. That driver looked my way. I turned my head toward my passenger and continued driving on the road, turning right at the light and then the next left.

As we were driving down the road toward his place, a car came up behind me with his bright lights glaring at me. I was scared. I kept my eyes focused on the map and where to turn. The passenger was living in a hotel. I pulled in, and the car behind me kept going down the road. I apologized to the rider because he appeared shaken, as well. I retrieved his chair out of the trunk and set it next to his seat. He transferred himself into the chair and thanked me for bringing him home safely. I made sure he couldn't see how scared I was.

When I saw he was in his room, I drove to a well-lit parking lot and pushed 9-1-1 on my cell phone. I spoke to the city police and then to the state police. I gave them the details, and then I drove home. It took me thirty minutes, but I felt safe as soon as I locked the door.

A few days later, I saw a black car at a gas station on the other side of Charlotte. I almost stopped in to check its license plate but then decided to keep driving. Sometimes I need to remind myself that I'm not a detective.

* * *

I've had two small collisions with my back bumper. The first driver stopped and apologized for not stopping quick enough. It was bumper to bumper on the interstate outside of the city. My car wasn't damaged, and I made sure my passengers were fine. I ended up hugging the other driver to calm her down.

The second incident was on Sugar Creek Road near the railroad tracks. I stopped to let an oncoming car turn left, and the driver behind me wasn't watching and hit me. I pulled over on the other side of the tracks, but he kept going. There wasn't any noticeable damage to my car. And I didn't have any passengers during that one.

* * *

I wish I could blame it on the rain and the foggy back-up camera in my car, but the accident was my fault. After dropping a passenger off at his townhouse, I turned the car around so I could exit the way I came. That's when I saw the One Way Only sign. The road I needed to go on was behind me. Instead of turning around, I backed my car up the road. I was like "Mater" in the Cars movie. I was zooming backward until I bumped into something. I thought it was a tree. I drove forward, but the car felt stuck. I got out and saw that I backed my car into a parked truck. I got back in my car and was able to pull it forward. Again, I got out of the car to examine the damage. There was a big dent in my rear bumper on the driver's side. The area around the rim of the right front wheel of his truck had damage.

Here it was, at 11 pm in the rain. I knocked on the door of the townhouse next to where the truck was parked. I thought to myself, 'who is going to open the door this late at night?' No one did. I tried another door, no answer. So, I walked down to the townhouse where I dropped my passenger off and knocked on his door. Thankfully he was awake and dressed. I explained what happened, and he walked outside and up to the vehicles. He wasn't sure who the car belonged to either but said he would check the next day. I thanked him. Before leaving, I grabbed a sheet of paper and wrote down my name and phone number and an explanation saying that I was sorry for hitting the truck, and then put it in a zipped plastic bag and placed it under the windshield wiper. Hopefully, the owner of the car would see it there and then give me a call in the next day or so.

In the meantime, I went about the night with a few more rides and then went home. The next day, I received a call from the owner. He had already been to his garage and would send me the bill. They didn't have to replace his bumper, only another part. I contacted my insurance company, but because I was working at the time with my rideshare company, they wouldn't pay for the damage to either car. So, I paid out of pocket, in two payments, thanks to the truck owner. And my car remains with a dent until I have extra money to replace it. (Six months later, another passenger gave me a heads-up on where to purchase a used bumper and then to go to MAACO to have the painting done, plus they would install it for half of what the collision shop quoted. It pays to talk to people.)

* * *

There have been some close encounters, where a driver stops quickly in front, or a driver behind me is too close when I slow down. There was one episode when a feature of my car put on the brakes and stopped the car for me. Talk about freaky. I had a passenger in the backseat and had to apologize for my car. The feature is that the car will beep when it thinks I'm coming in too fast before slowing down. I can honestly say that I do not like that feature because when it stops, the car is in control of itself. Then it takes a few seconds to release the control back to me. Self-driving cars, I'm not ready for them.

CHAPTER 4 - DIVERSITY

Charlotte is a diverse city, full of people from all walks of life. The company I drive for is LGBTQ friendly, which I love. I meet a variety of people across the gender spectrum from very masculine to very feminine and everywhere in-between. I love it when a couple admits they are partners or married couples. I make sure I tell them about the books I have written with the genre – gay Christian. Some told me that it's needed, especially for young adults. Everyone needs to know that God loves them no matter who they are, where they live, or whom they love.

* * *

A drag queen sat down in the backseat. I smiled at her through the rearview mirror. I wanted to let her know that she was welcome in my car. She said she appreciated that because I might be surprised about the number of drivers who would refuse to give her a ride. I don't understand why people are afraid of drag queens. The men, who are not gay, love putting on "costumes" (female clothing and makeup) and entertaining others. Some recite poetry, while others sing. Whatever their talent, they perform.

* * *

Some people will shake my hand at the end of the ride, for being so welcoming to them. (It makes me feel good to know I'm doing something that is needed – and will make a difference in the world.)

* * *

I've considered having a notebook in the car for passengers to fill out what country they are from and what language they speak. I've met people from all over the world. Charlotte is like a tossed salad. The people are the toppings – they come in all shapes, sizes, colors, genders, and sexual orientations. I try not to prejudge anyone the gets into my car, even when I don't understand what they're saying. Then I think of the advantage of knowing two languages. Most of the foreigners I've met learned English as their second language. It's funny sometimes listening to them on the phone (not that I eavesdrop on purpose). Every so often, they will say a word in English. I suppose it's very common to do that.

* * *

One rider had on shorts, a t-shirt, and sandals when it was 44 - degrees outside. I happened to ask him about it, and he said, "Everyone complains that I'm not dressed properly for the weather. But I get overheated easily, so it's better if I wear shorts in the winter."

* * *

As you'll read in Chapter 7 – Geography, I've learned a lot about other countries. When possible, I ask the passengers about their home country. Unfortunately, I don't remember everything nor have the time to write it down during the rides. The cultures vary from country to country, yet in America, everyone gets along. Or that's what my eyes witness. There are even different cultures within the United States, and it's fun to talk about the different words, such as a grocery cart in Pennsylvania is a buggy in Georgia. When it threatens to snow in the South, the schools close. Yet in the North, they only close schools when the temperatures are below negative 30, even if they have feet of snow. There is no one place that's the same as any other, and that's what diversity is about, learning to live peacefully with others.

* * *

I picked up a group of people at the airport. They returned a rental car and needed a ride back to the theater where they were performing that evening. They were four of eight in the group who sang and danced with percussion and guitars. They spoke Spanish and a little English. The man sitting in the front sang a few notes. The ride was very entertaining. Their group is named the Tablao Flamenco, the Soul of Spain.

* * *

Ever been in an enclosed place with people who don't speak your language? When they talk, all you can do is smile.

CHAPTER 5 – EATING IN OR OUT

As a young mother and son were on their way home from the store, they shared how much fun they were having together during his spring break from school. She announced that she found an easy recipe using strawberries, that is high in antioxidants.

"Slice the strawberries and place them on parchment paper on a cookie sheet. Bake for an hour at 200-degrees Fahrenheit, and then turn them over for an additional hour," stated the mom.

Her son added, "They taste like candy."

One passenger works at a sandwich shop called "Which Wich." He said the specialty has turkey, ham, roast beef, pepperoni, bacon, three types of cheese plus veggies and a spread. I've seen several of these eating establishments but have not stopped to eat yet. The specialty does sound amazing.

One couple ate at an Italian restaurant called Flamma. They stated the food was very good, although the service was extremely slow. They added that it's a good place to eat.

A young woman was on her way home from work and asked if she could add a stop at a Taco Bell.

"Sure, no problem." I followed the map on the phone and pulled in the drive-thru behind several cars. The line was moving slowly. When we reached the order board, I put the backseat window down so the passenger could order. Then we waited. By the time we reached the pickup window, they were only taking cash for the items ordered. My passenger wanted to pay with her debit card.

The person taking the order forgot to give us that information, yet the restaurant couldn't make it right. We left the store. I offered to take her to a bank, but the time it took to sit in the line was too long, and she needed to go home. If I had cash, I might have offered to pay for her food. But I rarely have cash on hand.

✳ ✳ ✳

One of the first riders to eat in my car was a woman I picked up at her workplace. She told me she was running behind in the morning and didn't have time to pack a lunch. Then she was busy in her office all day and didn't have time to stop for a lunch break. She asked if I would stop at the McDonald's on the way out of town.

Of course, I would do that. After receiving the woman's meal, I drove toward her destination which was a thirty-minute drive. As I approached the interstate, I looked in my rearview mirror and saw her sitting quietly with her bag still folded closed on her lap. Knowing she was hungry, I mentioned that it was okay to eat in my car. She was relieved. I heard the wrappers as she unfolded her hamburger, and I was glad it was still warm enough to eat.

There are times when I wish passengers would ask first before eating. Though I've never refused anyone. I only hope they would take their empty wrappers, bags, cartons, bottles, with them.

* * *

One chilly evening, I picked up a young couple with a four-month-old baby. At their first stop, while her husband went into a CVS for a few groceries, the woman spoke about their Thanksgiving plans.

She announced she would be cooking her husband's favorite dishes in their hotel suite, including shepherds pie, macaroni and cheese, collard greens, turkey, ham, and Watergate salad.

She bakes her sweet potato pies from scratch, while her husband makes a sweet butternut squash pie. I was about to ask what time they were planning to eat but decided to remain quiet. They were inviting several friends over to share in their meal.

I also asked if she would accept dishes made by her friends, and she responded, "No, because I can only trust the ingredients I use." Then it's good that her friends trust her to do good things. I would if I had the chance to sit down for a meal with them.

CHAPTER 6 – FOOTBALL GAMES

I met two young men who were not able to enter the stadium because they had counterfeit tickets. They had spent $150 each on Craig's List. The one guy said that his wife was going to be upset. So, I suggested, "Tell her how much money you saved by not having to buy beer and hotdogs." He laughed and said, "That might work, thanks."

* * *

One night after the game, I picked up two women who walked a half-mile away from the stadium to save $50. Thankfully the ride was longer than I anticipated. We had plenty of time to talk about college costs. One woman stated that 80% of those who graduated with a degree is no longer in that field.

That made me think we should change the reason for going to college. Instead of making it their career choice, they might see it as something they'd like to be doing for the next five years. Find what piques their interest or a favorite hobby? Not many employees stay with the same job, for eventually, the younger generation takes over. People need options and opportunities to do what makes them happy. Going to a trade school for two years might be a better option for students.

* * *

I met a young man who is going to school to work as a chef. He says his dad is a doctor who also loves to cook. They have season tickets to the Carolina Panthers. For every home game, his dad makes a specialty from the opposing team's hometown. When they play Tampa Bay, they'll eat crab legs. When they play the Buffalo Bills, they eat chicken wings. His favorite is when the Panthers play against the LA Rams (who used to be from St. Louis) because they eat ribs. They set up a tent while tailgating and share their food with others around.

∗ ∗ ∗

I met a football fanatic for the Carolina Panthers. Not only was he wearing a jersey, but his suitcase had one for every day of his trip. He was traveling to London, England, to watch the Panthers play the Tampa Bay Buccaneers. He has season tickets for the home games. Though, he didn't call himself a fanatic.

∗ ∗ ∗

I usually miss the surges that happen after the games when everyone wants a ride at the same time. One night I was blessed with a 500% pay. What would have been around $17.40 was $87. And that was one ride. I remember the passengers. There were four young men. One of them in the backseat, sitting behind me, was drunk. I told him to let me know if he was going to throw up because I would stop the car and let him out. I didn't want to clean up after him even though the ride-share company gives you $150-200 for that type of accident.

He kept saying that he wouldn't do that to me. But I was hesitant to believe him because the roads we had to travel on to get him home. They were windy and hilly. I thought for sure I would hear a gurgling sound before having the time to pull the car over. As the young men were talking, I missed their turn into the apartment complex. It was late at night with very few cars on the road, so I did a big U-turn and was able to get into the correct lane. The young man crawled out of the car and stopped to say thanks for getting him home safely. He added, "I told you I wouldn't get sick, Miss Sue." The other young men said thanks, and then they went home.

* * *

Picked up a young woman going to the basketball, not football, game. It was about a 20-minute ride from her house. We got about three miles away when she realized she forgot the tickets. So, what might have cost her $9, cost her $26. I felt bad, though it did improve my income.

* * *

The trickiest part about dropping people off for the football game is the streets close near the stadium. Passengers don't mind walking an extra block to the stadium, but they'd don't want to walk anymore after the game. I've had several rides cancel because I couldn't get to them in time.

There are designated pick-up spots, but the traffic in that area gets jammed, and so it's always better to call the passengers and give them another location.

One chilly night, a man called, and we coordinated a pick-up spot. We stayed on the phone the whole time as I was maneuvering around the city streets. When I finally reached them, the man got into the backseat while a woman sat upfront. It was his mom. She reached over and put her hands on my cheeks.

"Mom, what are you doing?" gasped the son.

"Oh, she's a woman," responded his mom, "she understands what it's like to have cold hands."

I laughed with them even though it was an awkward moment. The man apologized for his mother.

I turned the heater up in the car and took them to their destination.

CHAPTER 7 - GEOGRAPHY

This chapter lists the places my riders have lived or visited along with several interesting facts.

* * *

A woman born and raised in Iceland says that it's the best place to see the Northern Lights, that is, in the wintertime. But since it is so cold that time of year, she said it's better to stay at home and watch a YouTube video. She said you get the same effect without frost-bitten toes.

This woman is an airline attendance and has flown everywhere in the world. She resides in Florida. She added that after she retires, she has no desire to go anywhere else. At least, not beyond a 12-hour flight.

* * *

I met a couple from Chile, which is not to be associated with the chili pepper, although the shape is similar. On the southern end are glaciers with mountains to the east and the ocean to the west. The capital Santiago has over 7 million people, and other known cities have about 500K. There's even a desert there. They spoke about the food and mentioned one that is rolled up and folded over. It might be an Empanada.

* * *

Two couples who attended a wedding at the Botanical Gardens in Charlotte. On the ride to their destination, the man sitting in the front said he was from the island of Grenada, which is only 30 miles wide. They grow vegetables, get eggs from chickens, and milk and cheese from goats. Plus, the islanders' fish and eat seafood. The man had a full beard, and his body was fully tan. He looked like the salty Captain you'd see on a lobster boat.

✳ ✳ ✳

One passenger from the airport was getting home from a trip to Dubai. He said he'd been there eight or nine times for business. He said it's very expensive to eat and stay there. I admitted that Dubai is the answer many young people give to my question, "If you could go anywhere in the world on a dream vacation, where would you go?" He was surprised. I told him it's because there is gold everywhere.

✳ ✳ ✳

One of my riders from Colombia, South America, has been in the US for 15 years. The young man and I had a great conversation as he shared about his country and how beautiful the scenery is, along with tourism. He gave me a list of products that come from there, such as crude petroleum, coal briquets, spices, fruits, nuts, trees, steel, and iron.

I said, "Don't forget about the coffee beans even though I don't like coffee."

He responded, "I don't like it either."

In Saskatchewan, some say you can put a feather in the ground and grow a chicken. They call a hoodie (sweatshirt), a bunny hug. And in the summer, the temperature reaches 100-degrees.

* * *

There's a smaller island near Hawaii, known as a Polynesian island, that has a small tribe of indigenous people. They live off the grid – in huts covered with banana leaves, straw, and other leafy flowers. They cook over a fire. There is no refrigeration system or other "so-called" necessities.

There are dangerous tribes on the smaller islands. One young man who shared this information moved to the USA when he was six years old. He added that it's a very dangerous place that doesn't allow outsiders or tourists. He said he'll never go back to that type of living.

* * *

I met a man who was a boat captain and sailed around the world three times. It was a working boat where everyone on board had jobs to do. He said people don't want to live and work on boats anymore; they want to travel on cruise ships and sit in lounge chairs.

* * *

A van in Switzerland is called a "people-carrier."

* * *

Children in many foreign countries are taught English along with their native language. Some countries, such as Honduras, are tri-lingual, adding either French or Portuguese with Spanish and English.

Although there is danger in some countries, my passengers who were returning to their country, stated they lived in a safe part of the city.

CHAPTER 8 – HOMELESS ENCOUNTERS

There are more than 2000 homeless men, women, and children in Charlotte, NC. Although there are often not enough shelters for everyone, some choose to live in tent cities, sleep on city benches, or at door entrances. During the day, you might find them on the side of a busy road or at the end of an off-ramp from a highway. They have a hand-made sign that reads: Homeless. Anything would be appreciated. God Bless You. (Sometimes it says: Homeless Veteran.)

My church supports a group called the Watchmen of the Streets. They go out every other Tuesday night to hand out food, flashlights, sleeping bags, tents, and other needed items for the tent cities. During those hot summer nights, they'll walk down the main road to hand out water bottles. Each person has their own story of how they landed on the streets and what they're doing to get back into an affordable living space.

✳ ✳ ✳

I met a homeless woman who spent six years in the same location because God called her to move out of her home and into the street. The woman had a way about her as she was talking to my friend. While he hesitated to answer, she tilts her head upward and said something like, "Lord, I've got this."

I've been thinking about our conversation. The woman asks, "What do you see when you look at me? Where do you see God among my things?"
She added, "God is all around, He's here and there, and in you and me. He's taking good care of me and gives me what I need."

Her faith was huge.

She's still on my mind. I know when you experience time alone with God, He can do amazing things in your life. He is within an arm's reach. It's like the doors in your heart and mind are open to receive Him fully.

The same woman created a shelter using several tarps strung up and held by a tree branch and the side of some metal fencing. Inside were her worldly possessions, such as clothing, shoes, and bedding. Perhaps she has a box of canned food, as well. Her shelter was close to the transit train, which made it easy to find her.

One Sunday afternoon in December, a friend and I stopped to visit. We had been there several times before, but this time, my friend had purchased some items he felt would be useful for the woman, including a gift card to a local grocery store.

As we closed in on her made-up home, there was a dark green plastic chair off by itself, and she was nowhere around. We looked up and down the street before spotting her coming toward us from across the lot. The fencing that held her side of the tent was gone. She reported to us that the city would be building an apartment home in that spot, and soon she would have to move when we inquired where she said that only God knew.

This woman told us, on our first visit with her, that God wanted her to live outside. She had adult children who lived in houses but felt it was her calling to be outside on the streets. Neither my friend nor I have been in Charlotte for more than a few years, so that we couldn't verify that.

After the initial hugs, my friend handed the woman the gift bag. She tried to give it back.

I spoke up and said, "God laid it on his heart to give you these gifts today."

She immediately responded, "Well, God told me not to receive any more gifts from anyone. He is moving to me soon to another place, and I can't take anymore with me."

We were both shocked by her response. She went on a tangent and talked about how she loves both Satan and God, and they're both fighting for her. At one point, she says her husband is coming in a car to get her and take her home. But when we ask where she's going, she says only God knows.

"Do you have cancer?" I asked.

"Why do you ask that?" she responded.

"Well, you talk about going someplace with God, and I know that sometimes people die from cancer and then live with God in heaven."

And then came her speech. "Well, no, I don't. But those who are sick with cancer or have an illness, they die because they don't have enough faith in God."

I interrupted. "My husband had great faith. He was a strong Christian man."

She'd kept repeating herself, saying that his faith wasn't strong enough because of the spirit within him. He was fighting his own battle with God and Satan. (Suddenly she knows my late husband?)

I stood still, letting her talk even though her words stung. But I knew that if I kept giving her more information, she was only going to keep on talking. The only way I knew to get out of the discussion was to pretend that I agreed with her. I was polite. I didn't want her to keep saying that my late husband wasn't right with God.

My friend stood by trying to understand what she was saying. She was creeping into my personal space, and I would keep stepping backward. Sometimes she spits a little while she talked, and I had to wipe my face. I wanted to walk away (but that would be rude.)

Finally, I said, "Thank you for being God's messenger,"

And she added, "I hope you know that God told me to tell you these things so you would understand, to have faith and have the Holy Spirit in you."

"Thank you," I said. And in my head, I said, 'This was not the conversation I was expecting today.'

And I added, "I hope you will accept the gift that Allen brought."

She gave me a big hug, and then patted Allen on his shoulder. I could tell he was baffled by this conversation - as I was.

As we drove away, I told him that I had to agree to disagree with putting an end to the discussion.

✳ ✳ ✳

It's not until you meet someone who has next to nothing when you realize how blessed you are. I met a homeless man who stopped at my church to receive a Christmas gift – a new sleeping bag, tent, and some canned foods. As I left the church, I saw him walking down the sidewalk. I decided to extend an act of kindness and invited him into my car to take him where he wanted to go. On the way, I asked if he wanted something hot to drink, like a coffee or cappuccino. He said that would be nice, so I stopped at a 7-Eleven and bought him a hot coffee, a muffin, and an orange. That's all he wanted. I felt like I should give him more and even thought about bringing him to my place so he could at least be warm for one night. But I knew that would be awkward, as I hadn't met him before then. I dropped him off at a private area set up like a small camp. At least I knew he would be warm protected by the wind, though it was to be in the low 40's on Christmas night.

This small adventure made me think of the Christmas story, and glad God is with this man, as He was with Mary and Joseph that night. Prayers for all who are stranded or not able to have a place to call home.

* * *

I started carrying small packs of peanut butter and cheese crackers to give to the homeless people on the street. There's only so much change in my car, and I remembered my friend who volunteers told us that it's better not to give them money, for there are plenty of services available in the city for them to eat or get the things they need. Every so often, I hand out change or single dollar bills.

One day as I drove up to a red light, there was an older gentleman with a sign seeking money. I rolled down my window and tried to hand him some cheese crackers. He yelled back, "I don't want no crackers, Cracker!"

Well, in one moment, I was refused and insulted. But I let it go. Some people don't want a specific handout unless it's what they want – cold hard cash.

* * *

Another time, a pregnant woman was at the end of an off-ramp from the interstate. Her face was dirty, and she had a tank top on. She appeared to be at least seven months pregnant. I felt bad for the baby, so I gave her a few dollars. Although I've heard of people pretending to be homeless by begging for money, sometimes it's hard to tell the difference. So leave it up to God to decide how they're going to spend it.

* * *

It's also sad to see skinny dogs with homeless people. That's when you hope they use the money to feed their dog, too. But you wonder, are they using the dog to get more money? Thankfully, I haven't seen anyone with their kids asking for money.

* * *

Oh, wait, there was a time when I was at the movies with my grandkids. A woman and her child approached me. The woman said their car had broken down and they were from out of town and needed to buy a part for it. I gave her a couple of dollars. My grandkids were watching me. It was time to leave an impression and then talk about it. I told them there are times when I'm not sure whether to give or not, but I need to leave it up to God to decide. I'm doing what He wants – and that's to serve others.

* * *

I often stop at QuikTrip for gasoline and a pit stop. There are times when I'm also buying something to eat. One day I bought a hotdog. On my way back to my car, a man approached me and told me he was hungry and wanted some money to buy a couple of hotdogs. I offered him the one I had; that is, I offered him a hotdog. But he refused and walked away. I will note here that there was an ABC Spirit store next to the gas station – where you can buy alcohol.

* * *

Another time at a different QuikTrip, a young man approached me looking for some bus money. (It's a good thing I don't usually carry a lot of cash with me because I do have a kind and giving heart. It is hard to say no.) I gave him some loose change, and then he approached others asking for money. He came back to tell me that he missed the bus. Was that my fault? No.

* * *

Sometimes I think it's my shiny blue 2017 Corolla that gets homeless men to ask me for money. But I don't often carry cash.

One day I was at the grocery store a few days before Christmas. A man approached and said he wanted to have a nice Christmas dinner. He wanted to have a steak and asked me to give him the money so he could have one. I said, "I'm not even having a steak for dinner."

I pointed out some yogurts in my cart I had just bought and offered them to him. But yogurt wasn't what he wanted. He kept asking me for money, so I said, "Let me put this food in my trunk, and then I'll see if I have a couple of dollars to give you."

"Can I have $16?"

"No," I answered.

"Then, can I have $8?"

"Even if I had $8, I'm not giving it to you. Here's $2. That's all I have to give."

And he took that money and walked away. I put the cart back and drove off. I saw him over at another car, asking someone else for money. I told a friend about this, and they said he was probably looking for money to buy drugs.

* * *

Although I slipped up once or twice, I do know that it's good to acknowledge the person on the street by looking at them in the eyes and mouthing, "I'm sorry. I don't have anything to give you." That's one way to show respect without giving them something.

* * *

I gave a man an apple one day, and he was very thankful.

* * *

I made the mistake of buying two dozen Krispy Kreme donuts – the regular glazed ones. I ate four as I was driving toward home. They were still warm and tender, and the newly formed sugar flakes fell from the donut onto my shirt. I tried to pick them up and stuff them into my mouth, but of course, they crumbled more. I had to brush them off.

The next morning, I looked at the boxes on my counter and then proceeded to stuff two more donuts into my mouth. "How could they make them less tempting yet so delicious?"

I decided to put the remaining four into the other box of 12 and freeze them. That way, anytime I wanted a nice warm donut, I could zap it in the microwave for 15-20 seconds, and sooner than that, the donut would be in my belly. Into the freezer, they went. It was a Sunday morning. I showered and got dressed for church and decided I didn't need the temptation in the house. I grabbed the box and headed over to Tryon Street, where I knew some of the homeless people gather. I drove up, put the window down, and asked if they would like some donuts. There was no hesitation. I thanked them for taking my temptation away as I drove off. Whew. It's hard to give up something you love.

* * *

It's a joy to meet people from all walks of life, along with learning about our differences and hearing their stories. But, to be honest, I got slightly nervous when I saw three black teenagers approach my car for a ride. It wasn't anything they said or did, but a terrible stereotype playing in my head. I had already judged them as troublemakers before they got in the car. Having this perception about them upset me because I don't like it when others make judgments about me as a gay Christian. At least I was able to recognize my hidden prejudice before refusing them a ride. I do my best to love and accept everyone, no matter who they are or where they live.

By the end of the ride, I sensed they were nice kids. I was surprised when we ended up at the courthouse. I said a silent prayer as they exited the car, hoping everything would be okay.

The entire experience has proven that I always need to be aware of my thoughts and be sensitive not to prejudge others. I would want the same consideration. Perhaps we all need to give others the benefit of the doubt and look past their outward appearance before forming an opinion. We should take the time to truly get to know them — their heart and their mind.

See something, say something. That's what I did one day in February as I drove down the main road in Charlotte and saw a woman wearing a winter coat that had a fur hood around it. She was walking along the curb and peering into parked cars. At times, she stepped into the street to look inside the driver's side of the car. I couldn't tell from where I was watching if she was trying to open the cars. But I had heard that's what some of the homeless community does when looking for something of value. Instead of calling 911, I decided to flag down a police officer, for surely there would be one in town. I drove several blocks before spotting a squad car on a different street. When I caught up to it, I waved to get their attention. I rolled down my window and told them what I saw. And then they drove toward that area of town. I was curious to see if they found her but then decided to leave well enough alone.

CHAPTER 9 – IT'S A SMALL WORLD

This chapter relates how passengers have something in common with my family in places we've lived or visited. Or in knowing particular people.

* * *

I've discovered how small the world is. For instance, one of my riders recently visited my hometown in Pennsylvania. We're talking about Meadville, population less than fifteen thousand people. Another passenger knows the Golf Professional at the country club there. While others have been to Conneaut Lake Park or Titusville, home of the oil wells.

* * *

A passenger, also with the given name of Susan, says she's from a small town in Pennsylvania between Pittsburgh and Erie. I was trying to think of the exit number off Interstate 79 but didn't know it. She's from Cranesville, less than 30 miles from Meadville, where I grew up.

* * *

I was sharing with two young women about taking an Amtrak from Los Angeles, California, to Portland, Oregon. One of them says, "She's from Los Angeles, and I'm from Portland."

I love hearing people's stories and having the opportunity to share my own.

✳ ✳ ✳

One night of driving, I found something in common with everyone in the car. One person was from Los Angeles (My son lived there for 6+ years). Another was from Scranton, Pennsylvania, and worked at the ski resort where I skied one time with my first husband.

Others were from Phoenix and Philadelphia; I've been to both those cities. I met someone from New York City, where I was a small child. Plus, my dad grew up in Brooklyn.

I met a gay couple, and we talked about the need for decent conversations between the church and gays. The last two were from Chicago, and I always share how much my late husband loved Garrett's popcorn – the Chicago Mix flavor. We spent $75 twice by ordering two gallons of popcorn from Garrett's. I add that it shows how much I loved my husband.

✳ ✳ ✳

I had a surprise one day when I pulled up to a house, and my rider got into the car. It was a Facebook friend. We had met in person before that time, as well. She's a member of a Mama Bears Club, which is a group of moms with kids who identify as LGBTQ. She's the second person in almost 5000 rides where I have known the person.

✳ ✳ ✳

I met a woman who graduated from Allegheny College (in my hometown of Meadville). Another family was from Greenville (about

30 miles from Meadville), and yet another from Beaver Township, just north of the Pittsburgh airport.

* * *

I spoke with a man about sailing, which brought memories to my mind. I used to crew with my dad and brother during some races on Pymatuning Lake, near Jamestown, Pennsylvania.

* * *

It's a small world when you randomly pick up someone who goes to your church. He was dog sitting for a couple he met through a pet agency. The couple spoke highly of our church to my friend because of a rideshare driver whose name was Sue (me).

When I drive past the church, I always tell the passengers that although it looks like an old church, it's full of millennials who love the Lord. The church is Missiongathering Christian on the corner of 15th and Caldwell Streets in Optimist Park.

* * *

I drove a man to the airport. He was originally from Holden, ME. I have vacationed in Maine, so we talked about moose and other things.

He was telling me about how the moose population has decreased due to the ticks. Sometimes he would come across a moose laying on the ground suffering and would have to call the game warden to kill it.

He said they used to give out 4000 tags each year, but now they only give out 2000.

I told him about the time my late husband Barry and I drove 300 miles around Maine looking for moose. The only one we ever found was named Lenny, which is a solid chocolate moose in a candy store in Saco. (He hadn't heard of Lenny.)

As we approached the exit, I asked him if he knew about the airport overlook, and he said no. I told him my parents would have called it 'watching the submarine races.' He laughed. Then I pointed to the road that would take him there. He thanked me and said he'd check it out when he returned. I reminded him to take his wife.

A tired young woman who had finished her 3rd shift job sat quietly in the backseat. She was anxious to get home to sleep. I glanced at the destination, and it looked familiar. "I used to live on the street," I said quietly. – Treva Anne Lane. I turned the corner and pulled alongside the curb and instantly recognized the house as the exact one I lived in with my daughter and her family. I'm not sure why the house number didn't immediately register but seeing the house did. What are the odds of that happening in a city with thousands of people?

* * *

A rider on a short ride was impressed that I write about gay Christians. He shook my hand and thanked me as he got out of the car. He encouraged me to keep writing.

* * *

CHAPTER 10 – JUST SAYING I'M SORRY

Last night on my way home, I made a right turn on red (after a complete stop), and suddenly noticed a car to my left. He was honking at me, and I shrugged my shoulders and waved my hands - as if saying - sorry, I didn't see you.

Well, at the next red light, he rolled down his passenger window, and I rolled mine down. He yells, saying that I was supposed to yield to him and that I was in the wrong. (I couldn't get a word in) He went on to say, "I don't know why you're cussing at me."

And so, it was my turn. "I wasn't yelling at you. I was trying to tell you I'm sorry. I didn't see you."

And then he was like, "Oh, okay." He rolled up his window and went on his way.

I suppose that could have been uglier – if the man got out of his car and approached me. I'm sure I would have run the red light if that had happened.

I think he might have come up to the intersection fast to avoid the red light that was turning for him. He was turning left - as I was turning right. He wasn't at the intersection when I turned.

✳ ✳ ✳

It took me an extra 5-8 minutes to get to my next destination. A man from Norfolk VA got in and explained he was saving money staying at a hotel outside of the city. As we started on our way to uptown, he wondered why I wasn't driving on the interstate. I reminded him that due to the time of day, the highway would be full of cars, and we were on the best route to the basketball game. He continued to complain about taking city streets. I was close to losing my temper. But I kept cool and repeated that we were on the fastest route.

I pulled up to the arena (stopping where the pin was on the map). The passenger remarked that the main entrance was on the other side of the building, where you get tickets. I told him there was another entrance up on the right across from the bus station, but he wanted to go to the other side. I offered to take him but explained with the one-way streets that it might take another fifteen minutes, so he decided to walk.

I was surprised the roads were good as I passed him on the other side of the arena after picking up my next passengers.

✳ ✳ ✳

I gave one of my passengers some tips on how to deal with grief. His dad had recently died, and it was two years since his brother passed away. He said he wasn't close to his mom but was trying to be there for her. I shared with him that grief was different for everyone. Some people tend to keep their emotions to themselves, though when the tears come, it's best to let them out. Often people stay busy with activities because that helps the time to go by faster. I pray he finds a mentor or a close friend to listen and pray with him.

✳ ✳ ✳

I'm sorry I didn't give the girl a ride. I received a ping to drive 17 miles away from Charlotte – down to Rock Hill, South Carolina. I pulled up to a hotel and waited five minutes before calling the woman.

"Hello?" whispered a woman.

"Hi, this is Sue, your driver. I'm near the registration door of the hotel, where would you like me to…"

"Who is this?" That was a man's voice.

"Someone with this number ordered a ride."

"No one here did that. Get the f*ck out of here."

And I immediately hung up.

I felt a wave of sadness as I drove home. Did I do the right thing? Should I have stopped at the registration desk to report that phone call? I sent an email message to my rideshare company about it – and that maybe it was possibly an act of domestic violence or sex trafficking. I hope someone else was able to investigate.

Two ladies rode with me - they were going to the convention center. They noticed the estimated time of arrival was 8:37 am. I asked them what time they had to be there. They smiled and said, "8 am."

I returned their smile, stating the obvious that they wouldn't be arriving on time.

* * *

CHAPTER 11 –KINDNESS ACTS

Wild goose chases can be exhausting. But when you return the lost iPhone, it makes it all worthwhile. I found the apartment complex and the place where she got out of the car. It was 10:30 at night, but I figured, whoever forgot it, would want it back as soon as possible. So, I began knocking on doors. I finally found the woman who was my passenger. She was on the third floor. It was not her phone.

I got back into the car and scanned the app for another rider who could have left the phone. It was back in Ballantyne, which was at least another 20 minutes away. I remembered the neighborhood but couldn't remember the street. I thought about what the house looked like and where the driveway was in comparison to the front door. But several of the houses looked the same.

I pulled into a driveway, knocked on the door, but no one answered. It wouldn't be a night when people would be receiving pizza deliveries at 11 pm. Never wanting to admit that getting help would be a better solution, I finally checked my phone and discovered an email about a passenger who had lost a phone, complete with a contact phone number. I called and told them I was in their neighborhood. They gave me the correct address, and I was there in less than a minute. I returned the phone, and the woman was ecstatic because she was flying home to California the next day and wouldn't have been able to pick the phone up at the rideshare hub here in Charlotte.

* * *

Drivers receive a $15 reward for returning a lost item found in the car. It helps if the passenger reports something missing, to receive the tip. I've returned two umbrellas, a pair of gloves, several phones, and sets of keys. Sometimes the passengers will give cash tips, but usually, they add the tip in the app.

✳ ✳ ✳

Picked up a young man (in his late 20s to early 30s) - he was heading to a get-together but told me that he and his brother are driving down to South Carolina today (12/24) to surprise their mom for Christmas. Both brothers are chefs - so they're bringing the food to prepare the meals.

✳ ✳ ✳

I picked up a young man at the airport who was coming home to surprise his mom for Christmas. She had no idea, whatsoever, that he and his siblings were going to be there.

As it was, she had invited other friends to spend the holiday with them. The young man had to call each person and explain why they couldn't come without his mom knowing the real reason. Thankfully, his dad was in on the surprise.

I suggested he videotape his mom's response. Maybe it would go viral.

It was sort of funny when the man found out that his brother wasn't coming the same night as previously thought. He was like - 'who am I going to go drinking with tonight?' I guess he spent the evening with his parents instead.

✳ ✳ ✳

I heard the best true story on K-LOVE Radio (while working as a rideshare driver). A high school volleyball team in California lost their school to one of the forest fires. They had a game in another town and decided to go and play, even though they didn't have their uniforms or shoes.

When they arrived at the opposing school, they were welcomed by the other team who had made them shirts with their numbers on them and gifted them with kneepads, socks, and even shoes.

After the match, they invited the team to have dinner with them and presented each player with a $300 gift card. Plus, they were able to raise sixteen thousand dollars to help the team and school.

I had tears falling out listening to this awhile ago.

No matter who we think our "opposing team" is - we can still be blessed by them.

As a driver, I tend to go out of my way at times to make a passenger's day. There are times when I mess up and want a do-over. One night, I was getting rides in the same area, driving back and forth between two towns. I drove a young man home from work and then turned around to pick up a young woman and drop her off at work. My third rider was a young woman whose destination was 20 minutes south. As she climbed into the backseat, she announced that there was a phone stuck in the cushion. So, with that passenger's permission, I was able to go back to the pizza place to give the phone back to the young woman.

I went inside and looked around, but I didn't see the girl. I went to the counter and explained the situation, and another worker took the phone and said she would make sure my passenger got the phone.

Halfway down the road to the next destination, I received a text from the rideshare company that a male rider had left his phone in my car. I had a suspicion it might be his, as I never confirmed it with the girl. I quickly used Google to locate the pizza place and called to ask about the phone. They were able to call its owner who wanted them to return it, but they couldn't leave the restaurant. I told them to give me a half-hour or so, and I would be in to pick it up.

The traffic was terrible on the two-lane road, both ways. It took twice as long before I was able to drop off the girl and then another 30 minutes to pick up the phone and at least 20 more to return it. By then, I was able to call the young man and keep him posted on when to expect to receive his phone. He was glad to have it back in his hands.

I could have taken the phone into Charlotte and left it at the rideshare hub for the passenger to pick up. But I felt like since I was in the area, I should try to get it back to his rightful owner. Thankfully, I was able to do that.

* * *

A young woman was going to get her nails done because they were having a celebration/going away party for her 18-year-old cousin who was going to boot camp. We were talking about how some people have it in them to go and serve our country. I told her that it wasn't something I ever wanted to do, but I would gladly cheer on someone else. She said that was her, too. I made sure to tell her to let her cousin know that I thanked him for his willingness to serve.

* * *

I had the privilege of meeting a couple from Michigan. They flew into Charlotte and needed a ride to Matthews. She had several appointments with her oncologist since she was in remission from pancreatic cancer. (My dad died with that cancer, so I immediately connected to this woman.) After dropping her off at the hotel, I drove her husband to Zaxby's to get dinner, something gluten-free, since it was later in the evening, and she was too tired to go out.

During our short ride, I told him that I'd like to drive them to their appointments while they're in Charlotte. He was surprised but grateful. I gave him my number and told him I'd be there the next day. We had lovely conversations in the car. This couple was around the age of my parents (had they still been living), and so it felt right to do this kind of favor for them.

After their second appointment, I drove them back to the hotel to get their luggage, and then I drove them to the airport. I did all of this on my own time. They gave me their home address so that I could send her a note of encouragement. Her husband called a few months later and reported that she was in full remission and cancer-free.

* * *

Two young college men were on their way to a three-on-three basketball tournament, which raised funds to buy shoes for 100 kids. They also gave away two bicycles. That's an act of kindness.

* * *

A passenger knew a taxi driver in New York City that kept ten or more notebooks stuffed in pockets in the backseat. The books had stories and pictures entered by his passengers over the previous years. He encourages current riders to read or enter their stories during long trips.

CHAPTER 12 – LONG DISTANCE RIDES

Long rides can provide plenty of material to include in a book. One ride started at the Charlotte airport and was designated to end in High Point, NC. The rider was a single, 57-year old truck driver.

One story he told me was that he dated a woman for 12+ years and had three kids. Finally, he asked her to marry him. The kids were old enough to remember this. Three months after the wedding, he decided he had enough. He told his three boys that he had to leave.

He called his niece to get a ride, but instead, she called his wife, who met him at the house. He was trying to leave before she came home. He said, "I'm sorry, but I can't do this anymore." He left the house with his belongings and moved 20 miles away. He kept in touch with his children over the years.

He stated that he was so used to doing his own thing, that being in a committed relationship was too much work. He added that he currently has a sweet deal, living on a lake in the basement of a house and only paying $450/month. Our trip was 90 minutes long.

❊ ❊ ❊

One of the longer rides through Charlotte took about 35 minutes. I pulled up across the street from the house. After waiting a few minutes, I saw three or four girls walking out carrying duffle bags. It seemed as if they had a sleepover, and perhaps some girls decided not to stay overnight. There was another car parked in the driveway, but the girls passed that and proceeded to walk across the street. I popped open the trunk and got out of the car. The girls tossed their bags and other stuff, including a cool hoverboard, into the trunk. For it was Christmas evening. They climbed into the backseat, and I counted them. Not four, but five girls. The youngest sat on the lap of another.

Thankfully there was a mom with the girls. She was also an aunt to a couple of them. She apologized for having too many for my vehicle but added that the XL vehicle couldn't get to her until 1 a.m., and I arrived at 11:15 pm. I made sure they put seatbelts on, even if the youngest only had the shoulder strap over her. I looked at the map, and the directions were mostly on one road.

Things were going well until we reached this one intersection. We waited for what seemed to be five minutes, but the light wasn't turning green. We had witnessed a few other cars going through the red light, but I was hesitant to do that, especially because I was over capacity. I was behind two cars in the right lane (going straight, not turning). I was there a little bit, and one by one, the other two cars zoomed off to the right - only to cross over another lane to go through the gas station to get to the other side of the road (as if they were going thru our green light). Well, I sat there several minutes - and the light was not turning green. So, I said, to myself, here goes nothing. And I drove through the red light. There were two or three other cars still waiting for the light to turn green as I drove out of sight. At the next red light - we sat there for about a min, and it turned green.

The girls changed the radio station to a hip hop/rap music and turned the volume up - so as maybe to keep themselves awake before they got home. As we pulled into their apartment complex, I pointed to a sign that said: "Don't forget - the water will be turned off on 12/26 from 9 am-5 pm". The mom sitting up front was like - great - five girls and no water for showers. I was like - good luck with that.

✳ ✳ ✳

I've learned a lesson the hard way; I now call the passenger ahead of time to make sure they're not going to cancel when I'm on my way to pick them up. Especially when it's a long drive to get to them.

One ride to a pickup spot was thirty-eight minutes away (approximately 17 miles). The house sat on the edge of Lake Norman, north of Charlotte. Although he was a renter, he enjoyed having the use of a small boat chained to a wooden dock. Plus, he went fishing whenever he wanted. (I'd love to live on a lake and do those things.)

His ride was no more than fifteen minutes long. Sometimes it's frustrating to travel long distances for a short ride. My rideshare company has since changed and now pays for the time done toward the destination. At least it seems like a win.

✳ ✳ ✳

The longest ride to date was five and a half hours long. It started at the Charlotte airport. I pulled up to the curb and got out to help a woman put her bags in the trunk. I noticed that there was no destination listed on the app. She stated that her phone wouldn't let her put it in. I added it to mine. When I realized where it was, I asked, "So, you can't take a plane there?"

She answered, "My flight canceled."

"What about the train?"

"I have to work tomorrow, and the train gets in later in the morning, after I start."

"What about a rental car? I think that would be cheaper."

"I'm too tired to drive. I was in Jamaica for vacation, and I need to be home so I can work in the morning."

"Okay, I guess I'll drive you." The time was 8:30 pm.

The woman settled into the back seat, and we headed north on I-85. I stopped near Salisbury to fill up the car, and we both bought McDonald's meals for a late snack. I told her it was okay to eat in the car. Within an hour, the woman had settled in for the night. I could hear little snores. I turned my music up a bit and sang songs in my head.

The roads from Raleigh up to Richmond, VA, were quiet. Not many cars on the road, plus it was dark. I kept thinking about the money I was making. I figured that since I received $90 for dropping someone off 60 miles away, I should get at least $400 for this trip.

From Richmond to the Woodbridge exit, I traveled on I-95. The road was well lit, for there were more towns with gas stations, restaurants, and hotels off the exits.

I pulled into her driveway around 2:20 am. I woke her up, and she asked how much the trip cost her. I said that my app would tell me what I made, but I might be able to figure out how much she paid. So I selected dropped off, and my app read $235. I told her she would have paid around $315 or so for the ride. I retrieved her bags from the trunk and said goodnight. And then I was on my way home.

The home was six hours away. What was I thinking? I didn't want to spend the money I made in a hotel, so I decided to drive and then find a rest area or somewhere safe to park and sleep. The more I drove, the more I wanted to stop at a hotel. I started looking for one.

Every hotel I stopped at had a sign that read "No Vacancy." I told myself I could keep driving. But on the road, I was very tired. I had been out driving since earlier the previous day. I finally pulled into a Holiday Inn Express, and after seeing it's no vacancy sign, I climbed into the backseat and folded my sweatshirt into a pillow and closed my eyes. I slept for around two hours. It was not comfortable. I sat up and saw people leaving the hotel carrying briefcases and rolling suitcases. I got out of the car and decided to use the bathroom in the hotel.

The toilet needed plunging. So, I went into the men's bathroom, and then I stopped at the front desk to report the need in the women's bathroom. They thanked me. While I was standing there, the smell of scrambled eggs, bacon, and cinnamon rolls filled my nostrils. I made a quick decision to stay and eat breakfast and perhaps grab an apple for the road. I didn't rush, for that would make me look out of place. I went through the line like everyone else.

I did sleep (in the hotel parking lot), and so wasn't breakfast free for everyone? I was hungry. Anyway, I know that was wrong, but I'd do almost anything for one of their delicious cinnamon rolls. After I ate, I went back to the car and went on my way. I had to stop several more times, for two hours in the car doesn't give a tired driver much rest. I think I was home by 11 am.

I stayed home for the rest of the day. I decided that if I were ever to accept a long ride like that again, it would have to be in the daytime when I had plenty of rest and would be able to accept one or two returning riders. It has been quite a story to share.

The downside is that the woman forgot to give a tip.

✳ ✳ ✳

On the night of the eclipse, I chose to drive for my job instead of taking the day off to experience the event. I arrived at the Charlotte airport and picked up two young women heading to Greensboro. They asked if I minded driving the 90 minutes there, as some drivers prefer shorter rides. I agreed to take them. They put their luggage in the trunk and then sat down in the back seat.

They announced that their connecting flight had canceled and that there were no rental cars available due to everyone wanting to see the eclipse. One mentioned the idea of traveling by train but said it wasn't leaving until 3:30 am, and then it would make them late for work.

I told them that I was fine about taking them to the other airport, where their car was waiting in the parking garage.

They shared about their family and jobs, and then I gave them time to nap. When we arrived at the airport, I dropped them off. The girls gave me a $50 tip, which was very generous.

* * *

When an older-looking man sat in the front seat, he announced that I was taking him to Hotel California, which is when I learned that he meant jail. He said he had one more 24-hour day to serve to finish out his sentence. I think it was a car accident gone wrong. He didn't give any other details, which was fine.

He admitted he was 63 years old, but his wrinkled skin made him look older than that. He told me about the lung cancer he suffered through, yet he hasn't stopped smoking. Now he's trying to avoid having back surgery.

He shared why his hair was down to his elbows. He wanted to have it cut off to make a wig for a child who was dealing with cancer.

On the way, we talked about fishing and how he used to make lures. He said his favorite one was a plastic worm. He could catch all kinds of fish with it. He said he used to work for the electric company - burying cables mostly, but sometimes he got to climb the poles. When his daughter was sick, he quit.

Anyway, it was a great conversation. I asked a little bit about what jail was like (because I'm curious, but don't want to go there myself!), and the man said it's crazy at night because some of the men bang things against the wall and yell a lot. He sits in a cubicle all day. I asked if he got to do many activities, and he said no - that it's boring on purpose, part of the punishment.

When I dropped him off, he said if he had any money on his card, he would leave me a tip, but I told him that it was okay not to. I felt like his conversation was enough of a tip. It makes me want to drive out there tomorrow at eight and pick him up (but I won't). The ride that took me to Wingate was about an hour's drive from Charlotte.

CHAPTER 13 – MISCELLANEOUS PASSENGERS

There aren't too many days when I request not getting a tip. But this trip ended that way. While having a conversation with the passenger, I missed the exit. By the time I realized it, we were two and a half miles out of the way. I got off at the next exit and then cut through an old neighborhood to get to the other highway.

As I was going down the road, it was hard figuring out where the destination was. It was nighttime, and I assumed the rider was going to a hotel, so I headed for that. But then I passed the spot where the pin was on the map. I turned around in a Waffle House lot and told the man I was having trouble finding his location. Finally, I pulled up to a driveway near a chain-link fence. The man got off the car and disappeared behind the fence. I drove by a day or two later and saw that it was a junkyard with one small shed on the property.

Driving through a nice neighborhood with big houses, I turned to the rider and said, "This is a great neighborhood to look at Christmas lights."

He responded, "It is? I never noticed it."

I wonder if he notices now.

* * *

One afternoon I picked up two women and a little girl. One of the women was holding something close to her and had a jacket covering it. I didn't say anything about it, until that woman and the little girl was dropped off. That's when I glanced out my window and saw the cutest little white puppy pop its head out of the jacket. I told the other woman that I was fine with having the puppy in the car. I've allowed other dogs as well.

She said that some drivers would be upset because we're only to accept service dogs, so I told her next time to start a conversation with the driver and nonchalantly asked if the driver would mind if a non-service dog were in the car. Their response would tell you whether you introduce the dog or not.

* * *

When you think your car is nice and roomy, a young man sits in the front seat, and his knees are up against the glove box. You ask him how tall he is - and he says, 6 feet 7 inches. Yes, that was one of my passengers tonight. Another night, a man who was 6 feet 9 inches sat in the back seat, with the front passenger seat moved forward.

* * *

After dropping a student at Belmont Abbey College, I was pinged to go westward to Hickory Grove Road. It took ten minutes before arriving in the area. I drove back and forth on the road looking for the right mailbox number. But I couldn't locate it.

I called the passenger who told me he was the brother of the girl I was to pick up. He said she was in a house and so I went back to the closest address number and pulled into the driveway. It was narrow with ditches on both sides. There were no lights. There were two houses, one on either side of the driveway. Both appeared abandoned. Then further ahead, down a slope, was another building with its lights on. The brother asked if I could honk the horn. So, I did, several times.

For a moment, I felt vulnerable. Here I was on what could have been an abandoned lane. One of the dark houses was directly in front. I imagined the possibility of someone watching me out of their window, with a gun in hand. I was getting anxious and wanted to cancel the ride and drive home.

The brother called back and said, "Hang on. Either you're picking her up, or you're leaving her there. Let me get my sister on the line." Within a minute, I was talking with the girl. She asked if I was on Hickory Grove Road. I said, yes. She said she was at an apartment complex. I was baffled, for there wasn't one in the area. Then she told me she was near the corner of Sharon Amity and Hickory Grove Roads. "Sharon Amity? That's in Charlotte. I'm at least 40 minutes away. You'll have to cancel this ride so I can still get $5 for my time out here." But they said they couldn't cancel it on their side. So I did and didn't get any money for that fiasco. I went offline and drove the rest of the way home.

* * *

Earlier, I was taking a wealthy couple home. They were discussing how much to give the babysitter and came up with $100. For a minute, I thought I was in the wrong business. But then I remembered, kids drive me crazy at times. By the way, their ride was only $8.05. I felt slightly cheated. I let it go because I choose driving over babysitting.

* * *

Some might have thought I was blushing, but to be perfectly honest, my passenger asked me to turn on the heater. It didn't take long to feel the heat blast in my face as it tried to travel into the backseat.

It's not like she needed to get hot. She had a white sweater covering up a small top. She wore high boots with fishnet stockings and a polka-dot pair of mini-shorts. Surely, she wouldn't be cold.

As soon as she stepped out of the car, I turned off the heater and blasted the cold air over me. I felt like I was sunburned.

* * *

Most people are talkative, while others want to enjoy the quiet. I do my best to be respectful of what they seem to want (when they don't exactly tell me).

* * *

One of the young men that rode with me tonight said he didn't have any dreams of things he wanted to do. He asked me if that was bad. I told him that life is short, and we never know when our last day is. It's good to have done other things before that time comes. I added, let's say you write down 75 things you'd like to see or do, and then you do one of them every year. Then you know you've lived your life without regret.

* * *

Last night I took two rides full of "boys." One group were boys in their 20's, the other - men in their 40's. Each group was loud, boisterous, drunk, and a bit obnoxious.

The boys in their 20's were crude and rude - swearing loudly and saying things about sex I didn't want to hear. The young man who booked the ride sat upfront with me and kept apologizing for his friends' behavior. He asked them several times to downplay their cursing. To which - they responded with swear words. I did my best to ignore them, though it was difficult. The boy was afraid his friends were going to lower his rating, Maybe he'll learn not to travel around town with them anymore.

The men in their 40's were all about fun. They had grown up together since 2nd & 4th grades in DC - and two of them live in Charlotte - so they decided with the CIAA in town - it would be fun to get together. The man sitting up front was 6'10" tall. He was only going to be in the car for part of the ride because he had parked his own at a light rail station. The other three men squeezed in the back seat. The only married man with a child sat next to a door and fell asleep on the ride home.

As I pulled up to the parking garage, the tall man said he parked on the top level. I drove the car up. One of the guys suggested the man get out and take the elevator, but I spoke up and said I had never been in this garage before and wanted to drive him to his car.

They shouted, "Go, Sue!" I made sure no one was going to get sick as I made the sharp turns on the ramps. After dropping off the tall man, one of the guys from the back sat upfront. For the rest of the way to the destination, I shared some of the crazy stories as a rideshare driver. One of them asked if they were going to make the book. Perhaps they will. By the time I dropped them off, it was 12:45 am.

$$* \quad * \quad *$$

I had dropped off a university student at his dorm when I received a ping to pick up another less than a mile away. I drove over to the apartment complex and found the building number, though I have no clue which door the student will appear. I backed my car up to the far end of the building and then slowly pulled forward. I saw a couple of guys getting groceries out of their car, but no one who appeared to be looking for a ride. As I was about to call – the message appeared – 'Ride canceled.' I guess it wasn't because I couldn't find the person, but still frustrating to go somewhere and then not have a rider to take places.

* * *

Then there was a couple who had returned from a two-week vacation in Hawaii. I joked with them about still liking each other. When I pulled in their driveway, I suddenly wished I hadn't said anything, as I saw a sign that read: "Welcome Home, Mr. & Mrs." Before I drove away, I wanted to watch him carry her across the threshold, but he left her standing on the sidewalk with two large suitcases.

* * *

One young woman I picked up at the airport had come to Charlotte to visit some of her friends from college who were already married. She admitted that she enjoys the single life with the opportunity to travel. She told me about an upcoming cruise to Mexico that she and her friends were going on next year. She hopes everyone will be able to go.

* * *

Even though it tended to rain the very next day after getting my car washed, I decided to use it as an excuse to vacuum the car. It wasn't long until I had a nice shiny and clean car. The day was going well with compliments about how clean the car was.

The third passenger was a woman. We drove for 10 minutes and arrived at a church where her son had preschool. After buckling him in, I could hear the woman open a package of crackers and handed some to her child. The ride to their home lasted around eight minutes.

As she was getting him out of the car, I turned around to see crumbs all over the seat and floor, with some looking smashed, as if sucked on and then laid back down on the seat. I quickly handed her some wipes and asked her to clean it up. She got most off the seat but left some crumbs on the floor.

Thankfully, I didn't get any bad ratings for a messy car that day though it didn't help to find myself amid construction vehicles with dust flying everywhere.

* * *

One young man and I were discussing the rent situation in Charlotte. Many of the one-bedrooms start at $1200 per month. He said he found a penthouse that is only $4000 per month. He said he could rent it with three other friends. But I reminded him that some landlords require three times the rent in income from each person who is renting.

So, he and each of his friends would have to make a minimum of $12,000 per month. He was taken aback and agreed that it's a ridiculous rule, though we both understood the purpose of it. If one or two of his friends had to move, the remaining tenants would have to be able to pay the rent on their own. He decided not to apply for the penthouse.

* * *

I pulled up to an empty lot in front of a closed office. An older woman was leaning against a column. Out of the corner of my eye, I saw a man who was probably a doctor because he had a white jacket on over his shirt and dark slacks. He said he wanted to make sure the woman's ride arrived. Her first rideshare driver canceled when he couldn't find her. She said she called to tell them, and they hung up on her. I folded her walker and put it in the trunk. I tried to brighten her mood and said, "Well, that was a terrible April Fool's Joke to play on you."

And she responded, "That's right. It is April Fool's Day. Well, that wasn't a very nice trick."

I continued to tell her that not all drivers are nice. I've heard some say that if the passenger doesn't show up in the three to five minutes, they leave, canceling to get the $5 no-show pay. I think that's wrong.

* * *

I was outside someone's house waiting when I got a text saying they would be right out. I waited some more, and then the passenger called me. It was a mom saying that I was at the drop off place and not the pickup. She had put the address in the wrong spot on the app. So, I suggested she cancel the ride and schedule another one. That way, her son would get home sooner than if I went up to get him; it was a 15-minute drive one way.

So, she canceled. I sent an email to the driver support office and explained why I shouldn't receive the $5 non-show. They took care of it and thanked me for my honesty.

Putting the addresses in the wrong way is very common and is done most often when there are two stops.

* * *

Two high school girls sat in the backseat and had a very colorful conversation for the following thirty minutes. I heard several words that aren't in my vocabulary. They didn't want me to follow the GPS, and so I went a different way. They had me stop at a Dairy Queen to buy a quart of ice cream. The next time we came to an intersection, I stayed straight instead of turning, as the GPS suggested. I assumed they would question why I turned left when their ending point was straight ahead. But then they complained that it was taking longer to get home, due to the traffic on the main road. I didn't respond. I moved along the best I could on the road and eventually got them to a place where they could exit the car.

* * *

One of the male passengers was heading to basic training in a few months. He set several goals: - get a real estate license, get a dealer license (for cars), earn a degree in mechanical engineering with a double minor in computer science, and drafting. He wants to start a nonprofit to help young kids know how to dress for different occasions. He says he loves wearing a bow tie when he's not playing basketball. This man has plenty of ambition. I'm sure he'll accomplish his goals.

CHAPTER 14– NAUSEATED EPISODES

As I pulled up to the hotel lobby, the young man sitting in the front seat announced that he was going to throw up. I reached into the glove box and handed him a gallon-size plastic bag. By the time he had it up to his mouth, his insides had come hurling out.

He hadn't said anything about feeling sick during the fifteen-minute ride to the hotel. I suppose if I had known, I would have given him the bag ahead of time. Though listening to him, throwing up was making me feel sick to my stomach. I gagged several times, holding back my insides.

When he finished, he got out of the car and, thankfully, took the bag with him. I decided that the next time someone is feeling sick, I'm going to stop the car and let them get out first.

(I know my rideshare company would pay up to $250 if someone throws up in my car, but the thought of taking a photo of it and then taking the time to clean it or getting it to a car detailer, I would lose time on the road to make money. Besides, I have cloth seats in my car. It would be nasty!)

After arriving at a hotel, a young woman sat in the front announcing she married her best friend, that evening. We were waiting for her husband as another couple climbed in the backseat. Finally, he arrives and sits down behind his bride. It was strange that they weren't sitting beside each other.

The destination was to a nightclub in a busy music arts area. During the thirty-five-minute drive, they discussed if they were going to keep going or turn around and go back to the hotel. The bride and the other woman wanted to go.

The groom appeared tired and withdrawn, while the other young man complained of feeling sick to his stomach. Great. I turned my head and told him to let me know so I could pull the car to the side of the road to let him out. The census ended as everyone was going. So, we continued onward.

It was a very busy area. Lots of traffic going both ways. As I inched my way up the street, I heard a door open. I stopped the car, and the man behind me leaned out into the street and threw up. I was able to pass him some paper napkins to wipe his face. He then closed the door, and I moved the car forward. Another minute or two, everyone was getting out of the car and thanking me for the ride.

As soon as I was able, I stopped the car and checked the door. Thankfully, he had not thrown up on the door or in the car. I wiped the side of the door down with antiseptic wipes before another passenger entered the car.

A student finished track practice and was riding in the backseat to his home. He asked me to pull over because he was feeling sick. I was in the left turn lane on a four-lane road. I reached into the glove box and pulled out a plastic bag. He took it as I decided that my only option was to stop the car and put on the hazard lights. The student got out of the car and walked to the side of the road before bending over to spit up. He dry-heaved a second time and then got back in the car. The driver behind me wasn't happy about missing the green light, but I was glad not to have a mess in my car.

CHAPTER 15 - OCCUPATIONS

One of my airport passengers was a financial planner. He sat in the front seat and proceeded to share ideas on how to create more income. He said that to have enough money for retirement, you need to take half of what you make to live on and then put the other 50% in the savings. He said the less you can live on now, the more you'll have when it comes to retiring. I didn't have the heart to tell him that I was probably not going to retire. Since I spent over 35 years being a stay at home mom, it was going to take a long time to save enough to retire.

But I wouldn't have changed a thing in my own life. I enjoyed the flexibility to be home with the kids or go on school field trips with them. So, in this case, sometimes you learn to nod your head in agreement.

* * *

One question a rider asks is, what is my other job? I tell them that driving is my only work. It's something I've always loved to do. Plus, I can meet people from all over the world without leaving the Carolinas.

There are definite benefits I miss from having a traditional position, like time paid off or company-paid health insurance, or even having a company car because my 2017 Corolla is gaining more miles each week. It hit the 100,000-mile mark on September 21, 2019.

Driving with the reason to write books is my dream come true.

* * *

A 7-Eleven worker says that the late-night shifts are crazy, and I should never try it. That's when drunk people get out of hand.

* * *

Did you know that there's a company that manages the parking lots in town? They even hire the attendants for valet parking. It's called 'Preferred Parking.' I met a man who wanted to add another parking lot management in Charlotte, but I don't remember its name.

* * *

Recently I learned that the airlines are hiring people of all ages, even those in their '50s, '60s, and '70s. They see the older generation as more flexible and willing to work overtime or take unpopular flights. I was looking into becoming an airline attendant, but then when I watched the video, it showed them kneeling to practice on a CPR dummy. If I knelt, they'd be working on me, for I am too much out of shape to be kneeling, bending, twisting, lifting, or squatting. But if you need an announcer, I can say funny things.

One woman said, it depends on the airline, but their pay starts fifteen minutes before the door closes. Others don't start until the exact time the door closes. The same goes for the pilots.

Others say that it can be a fun and rewarding job if you don't go in to make a ton of money. One perk is friendship – your crew becomes like a family, especially when you work for the same flights.

* * *

I met a man who promoted to the general manager of a Chipotle restaurant. He had only been working there for a year. I congratulated him in that effort to work hard to obtain the goal he set out to achieve. I asked if he had been in the restaurant business for a long time, and he said no. He used to be a contractor, had worked for the water company, done some electrical work, and odd jobs. He said he was ready to pursue something new. He loves what he does now.

* * *

I picked up a man from the back of the airport - at the training center for American Airlines. He is the shuttle driver who takes flight attendants and pilots back and forth to the airport. It sounded like a great way to build relationships. Before working there, the man was a truck driver who drove up and down the east coast. He said it would have been nice to drive out west, now and then.

* * *

An interior designer, who does custom furniture, was in my car. Her company can design anything, right down to the type of arm on the chair or sofa, along with the type of material. They work with Ethan Allen and other furniture manufacturers, even the Amish in Pennsylvania. I guess having a sociology degree makes her job interesting - as she deals directly with the customers.

Being curious, I asked plenty of questions, which made the long ride interesting. The rider asked why (I asked questions) - and I told her, "well, I'm a writer - you never know when I might add a character in the story that does this type of work."

And then she said that she should write a book because of all her experiences. She says dealing with designers can be crazy. She had a title for her book - something like - "Buy it, B*tch." It was funnier when she said it.

* * *

One person works for TV - producing, writing, directing, etc. She can choose her projects and travels to different cities. I had the opportunity to tell her about my books, and she said she was going to read them. Wouldn't it be cool if someone wanted to turn it into a movie?

✳ ✳ ✳

A young woman attending Queens University was studying music theory with a possible minor or business.

"Music therapy works with people dealing with PTSD, Autism, mental health, nursing home patients, and school children," she stated.

When I asked what type of instruments she needed for this degree, she said, "the piano, guitar, ukulele, and a type of percussions like a snare drum or bongos. Voice lessons are also a requirement. Thankfully, I love to sing."

This passenger wasn't only taking lessons, but she was giving them to children and young teens after school. Her students perform recitals twice a year. This young woman became interested in music theory after writing a research paper about it in high school.

✳ ✳ ✳

Have any of my Charlotte friends watched the band called Sammie's? I gave William a ride one night.

✳ ✳ ✳

I met a third-generation chef who studied business management at Johnson and Wales University in Charlotte. He's from a family of nine. Two of his sisters are pastry chefs, another brother cooks. This young man wants his family to move down from the Bronx, New York, and start a family restaurant. He's already had one business plan looked at by a banker. Now he's making the adjustments and will probably start a restaurant before his family arrives. He added that even though his family is Italian, they also specialize in other European foods, as well.

* * *

Not too many people inquire about being an exotic dancer. This woman was surprised when I started asking questions. I told her I was a writer and that I'm always looking for details to share with others who are curious but are too shy to ask.

She explained that women are not permitted to go into the establishment without an escort. Otherwise, they would perceive them as someone who was trying to "steal the business or clientele.". When women do come in with a date, she tries to make them feel more beautiful than herself. She added that it could get awkward when a man becomes more interested in the dancer than his girlfriend.

* * *

I got the autograph of a young man who was hoping to go to Hollywood one day as an actor. He was working at Amazon to earn enough money to travel to California. I told him about a classmate who is a coach and actor in L.A., and I also informed my classmate, incase this man reached out.

* * *

I met a young woman studying to be a mechanical engineer. Her story was sad. She shared about her childhood of abuse and neglect, and how the foster care system was working. She admitted to having been in the system for four years before being adopted. She remarked on how frustrated it was to have people asking her how she was doing. She didn't want the teachers to point out that she was the foster kid or the one who was abused. She blamed herself for years over the death of her little sister. The police didn't show up at their house until her sister drowned. It was a very sad story, but the good part was that she has a relationship with God to remember how much He loves her.

* * *

I met the man who plays the pedal steel guitar for Kasey Musgraves. He had the day off before a concert, so I drove him to a local golf course. He travels all over the world with the band.

* * *

During the NBA All-Star week in Charlotte, the transportation administrator took a ride in my car. She's responsible for scheduling the rides for the players to and from the venues and their hotel. She admitted that it's a lot of work to plan, and you must be onsite for the event for those 'just in case' situations. [Months later, I gave a ride to someone who had also met this woman. That's a small world thing.]

* * *

I met a woman who is a cliff diver from a minimum of fifty feet up. Now that takes bravery.

* * *

A manager from CAVA, a Mediterranean restaurant, had subbed at one of his restaurants in the University City across the county. He had moved down from DC when there were 77 stores. Now they have over 300 and have recently acquired the Zoe's Kitchen restaurants. The one issue he brought to my attention was that the minimum wage in DC is $15 an hour, whereas, in Charlotte, it's only $7.50. He wanted to give his employees that wage but wasn't sure how to go about it because he realizes not everyone stays in business. So, I suggested he set a goal of three-five months where if the employee is still working hard, or doing more than expected, then that person would earn the extra hourly pay. He liked that plan.

I had a 26-year-old rapper in my car who was excited to get his business organized. He explained there are times when he needs to get permission from a professional rapper to use their music or beat to record his songs, so he doesn't plagiarize. Currently, he only has one song on YouTube, and it's called Party Paac – Alien Cheeks.

When I looked online, I recognized him right away because he had purple hair under his cap. He spoke about having five upcoming shows in Charlotte. Upon further questioning, he told me that he never writes anything down. He admits that it's easier to keep his songs from being stolen. When he goes to the studio to record, then it simply flows off the top of his tongue. Everything he raps is for his generation, the millennials. He doesn't have a special theme or even a special inspiration place. He adds that the songs just come to him.

He's fortunate to have a graphic designer in the family, his mom. She helps him design postcards and business cards. As far as earning money, he says it's going to take some time to get noticed, but in the meantime, he does earn a small amount of money every time someone watches and shares his YouTube video. Even when people say ugly things, he earns recognition. Good or bad reviews are always a plus for him.

✻ ✻ ✻

Two men wearing white pants and shirts walked up to my car. We exchanged names, and they sat down in the backseat. I asked if they were painters, but they replied, "No, we're bakers."

I said, "Even better because I love donuts and pastries."

They stated they make every kind of pastry that sells at the grocery store, even Krispy Kreme's. One admitted that he rarely eats donuts anymore after making them, but the other said he has a box on his kitchen counter. I thought maybe it would be a good place to work so I wouldn't eat so many of them, but due to my love for sweet things, it probably wouldn't work.

* * *

Earlier in the day, I gave a ride to a young woman who was excited about her new job at the airport. She would be cleaning out the planes in between the flights. I asked her what that meant she would do, and she said she didn't have any of the details.

The very next rider was a young man on his way to the airport to work. I asked him what kind of job he had, and he replied, "I clean out airplanes." What a coincidence. I asked him what that entailed, and he told me that two or three people would go on the plane to straighten the magazines behind the seats, look for any trash, and restock the bathroom with tissues, paper towels, and toilet paper. (I thought that would be an easy job, and the young man agreed.)

* * *

I talked with a young man who worked at Little Caesars.

I asked if he had dreams of making pizzas, and he said, "No, I dream about burning it down."

I followed up with, "How long have you been working there?"

"Three months. I don't want to eat another pizza."

"Have you worked in other fast-food restaurants?"

He said he did. He enjoyed working at Sonic the best but switched jobs to change things up. I bet he'll be going back. In another conversation, he said he'll be working a long time because his dream car is over $100K.

* * *

One of my riders was an oncologist. He was in town for one day to speak at the Levine Cancer Center. He said he was sorry to hear about my husband (who died from esophageal cancer in 2013).

He said that both esophageal and pancreatic cancers are death sentences because they have no prior symptoms, but researchers are working to find ways to identify it early. I was sure to say thanks for all the work he is doing for those who have cancer.

* * *

A traveling tattoo artist drives to the customer's home to perform the art. He admits it's a safer place for people who desire to have a tattoo on a body part not seen by the general public. People tend to be more comfortable in their own home while having beer or wine to stay relaxed.

When asked if it's easier to tattoo someone who has been drinking, the artist stated that he doesn't tattoo inebriated people for a couple of reasons. He said they're less likely able to sit still, and if they move around during the process and the tattoo blurs, the customer blames the artist (when they're sober).

The farthest the Carolina Tattoo artist traveled was to Miami, FL, for a whole-body tattoo. The fee includes all traveling costs.

* * *

The moment you find out your passenger is a fitness instructor, you suck in your stomach and hope they don't notice the rolls in your belly. Then you make up a believable excuse about why you're overweight along with your plans to start exercising. This man helps people lose weight through kickboxing. I kiddingly told him that I might run into him again someday. Then I clarified that it wouldn't be in my car. Of course, this is one of the funny things that take place as a rideshare driver.

* * *

A woman works for the Family Dollar Store. She said it's fun except she doesn't get any discounts or benefits.

* * *

I met a truck driver and learned information to share with others. He explained why semis don't have fenders. It's to protect your car if you accidently pull in front of them on the highway. The truck won't crush your car. By the way, truckers don't like it when cars do that, because they have the less stopping ability and, therefore, are more likely to hit your car.

While driving down a hill, the trucks shift in lower gears first before applying the brakes, because the more they use them (the brakes), the less productive they become. That's why you see runaway ramps off the highways for trucks who use their brakes too much.

* * *

A young man's destination was from one bar to another. I asked if he was going to a place where everyone knows his name. (Like the TV show – Cheers). He said they know him in both bars, but the one he's going to is the one his mom owns and runs.

I asked if he works there, but he said he was a chemical engineer.

"But isn't that similar to mixing drinks at the bar?" Of course, I was teasing.

He added that he does stop in every so often to help, especially when there's a party. It's not his dream job, only his mom's.

CHAPTER 16 – PICKING UP PEOPLE

As I pull up to a busy nightlife area in uptown Charlotte, there are orange cones placed between the lanes to encourage drivers to slow down. My GPS was directing me to turn right, but the road was blocked. So, I pulled off to the side and called my rider.

"Hi, This is Sue, your driver. The road is blocked. I can't drive to where you are. You'll have to walk to me. I am on the main road."

"Honey, are you from Charlotte?" asked a man.

"No, I'm not."

"Well, that's obvious. Now, honey, you need to find another way to come get us."

"I will try and find you. I'll call back if I have any trouble."

I drove up and down the street, but there was no other entrance to where he was waiting. The next thing I heard was a ping on my phone – Rider Canceled. I was relieved. I wasn't sure what he was going to say as he climbed into my car.

* * *

One night, I got pinged from a rider just up the road as I was turning left onto another street. I couldn't make a U-turn because it was a one-way street. I made the first left and then another left. I wanted to make the third left, but that street was blocked, as well. By the time I was a block away, the rider had canceled. Some days, driving can be very frustrating.

* * *

One evening I was summoned to the corner of South Tryon and 6th Street. I waited. No one approached my car. I called the rider.

"I'm at the Ale House," he said.

"Um, where is that? Is it on Tryon?" I asked.

"I don't know. I'm from out of town."

"OK – well, I will try to find you." I hung up and went around another block, coming up on 4th street. Although there are streetlights, it was still hard to scan the names of the buildings while also watching out for cars moving in and out of the lanes. Oh, and then also look for someone who needs a ride.

Incoming call from my rider, "Are you still going to pick me up?"

"Yes, I'm trying to find you. I'm sorry, but my GPS took me to Tryon and 6th. Can you give me another landmark?"

"Across from the Bank of America."

"OK." And finally, I pulled up and found the rider. He got in the car, and I apologized again for not locating him. He was from out of town but had lived in Charlotte years ago. (But didn't know the streets and landmarks any better than me,)

As I went to drop him off at his hotel, I said that I hoped he wouldn't give me a bad rating because the program had messed up the directions. He said, "Not a problem. Thanks for the ride."

✳ ✳ ✳

One day, I received a notice to pick up a passenger on the corner of 5th Street and South Caldwell. I wasn't too far away, so I turned right on 5th Street and drove down the street but didn't see anyone looking for a ride.

I called the rider, "I think I must have passed you. Where are you standing?"

"I think I'm on 5th Street." (Apparently, she wasn't sure herself).

I responded, "I'll swing by again and see if I can find you." As I drove up 6th Street, I got a ping –

A text message: 'Rider Canceled. We'll find you another rider.'

It didn't take long to get another ride.

* * *

When I pulled into a man's driveway, he asked if I could give him a ride and if I minded if he had a case of beer with him. I said it was okay if he gave me one. I was joking, but he didn't realize that. After the ride, the man opened the case and handed me a can. I thanked him and then thought about who I was going to give the beer to, for I'm not a drinker.

* * *

A young man with a pizza got into the car, and I drove him home. We had a good conversation about living where it snows. He went to Appalachian College in Boone, NC. There was a nearby ski resort where he learned how to snowboard. He admitted that he spent most of the time on the ground. He told me how much he likes snow and cold and hopes to move north someday, but not as far as Alaska. He was thinking of Michigan.

* * *

After reaching the pickup location, a man approached my car and opened the back door. I was about to ask for his name when another man came up behind him and said, "This is my ride." When I asked his name, he replied, and I knew he was my rider. The other man walked away.

* * *

Occasionally, passengers would sit in the back to be more comfortable and possibly to enjoy their music. One man had a splint on his right leg. He sat in the back with his leg up on the seat. He said he fell off his gas-powered scooter and broke his kneecap. Ouch.

* * *

A young woman was sharing that her mom announced that they're going to Hawaii - as a Christmas present. I said - I want to be in your family. I took her to the store and then back home. She said that her mom works for the airlines - that's how they got the tickets. She added that her little brothers' 10th birthday is at the end of the week, and when his mom asked him what he wanted, he said to go to Hawaii. I asked the girl what she got for her 10th birthday, and she replied, "Barbie Dolls." I told her she's going to have to start thinking bigger. She said – "Kids these days only want expensive things."

* * *

As I was coming up North Davidson, I got a ping – with an address. So, I slowly drove up the street, which had parked cars on both sides of the road. It's a busy place. I kept an eye on my GPS to see where the holder of the cell phone might be standing. When I didn't see anyone, I turned the car around but stopped briefly on the other side of the street. I was about to go when suddenly people were climbing into my car.

I checked to make sure I had the correct riders – and then we were on our way.

* * *

A young man works for a company that buys out mom and pop businesses that are struggling financially. Sometimes, it's because a spouse has passed away, and the business is too much for the one left behind. He said that one company tripled in sales not long after it was acquired, simply because it was now on the internet. Social media is the place to introduce your products.

* * *

A rider lives in a townhouse designed for four people. He lives in the master suite and pays half as much as I do for my apartment (which would be around $450). His home is in Mount Holly, which is about 30 minutes from center city Charlotte. Prices tend to drop the further away from the city, though that's not always the case.

* * *

I was blessed to give a married gay woman a ride home from the airport. Of course, I didn't know she was gay until she told me. (I share this to say it's more common than you might think - and I was happy for her.)

My riders often ask me what I do besides driving, so I'm always led to share my writing adventures.

And in the conversation that followed, this woman told me about her wife and how they adopted three foster kids (siblings) and gave them a wonderful place to grow up.

I think that's awesome. People who have the gift of fostering kids are heroes in my book. It takes a special person to open their heart to a child, knowing that most of the time, it breaks when the child leaves. That's a true saint! God bless those who take care of parentless children in the world.

∗ ∗ ∗

I offered three young men cold-water bottles, but they said they only drink alcohol. It was obvious they had started drinking before I arrived. We drove passed an adult night club, and they discussed what it would be like to manage a strip club with sand on the floor like it's on a beach. I suppose that would make things interesting.

CHAPTER 17 -QUIRKY OR QUESTIONABLE

An older man got into the backseat. He was lugging around a canvas bag full of groceries (big cans). He was a jolly older man who laughed at almost everything I said. First, he asked me what kind of car I had. I said - a 2017 Corolla with almost 62K miles on it. Hahaha

I told him this car has been on several long trips but mostly all over Charlotte. Usually, up to 200+ miles. Hahaha

I asked if he was ready for Christmas, and he said yes. I said I'm not celebrating this year, I mean, I'm not giving any presents because I don't have any extra money. Hahaha

You know, I said, I have peace about it because I have no stress from going into stores to figure out what to get everyone. Hahaha

(He's a man of many words. Hahaha)

I asked what the last car he drove? He said it was a Pontiac. And I said like 1978? And he said, 1980. You probably never heard of it, but it was an AMC. I said, yes, I've heard of it. He said it was a Pontiac Grand Am.

Then I asked if he used to be married and had any kids.

He said Hahaha

I guess that meant no.

Oh, and I asked if he's lived in other places besides Charlotte, and of course, he laughed. Hahaha

He said he lives in the same house where he was born. (I think this must be a rundown older house). I asked if he was holding out, waiting for the right price to sell (as many lots are being bought up with big new houses on them.)

He said, no, he hadn't given it any thought. (Oops, maybe he will now. Hahaha (that's me)).

We pull onto his street. I said, hey, you have neighbors, that's good. I pulled in the driveway, which is just grass and dirt. He said to stop and not go in any further.

He takes his time, and I can tell he's trying to find his wallet, so I turned on the light. He gives me a $5 tip. I thank him. Then he opens the door and carefully picks up the heavy bag and puts it outside, and then he slowly gets out. It seems as if the bag was going to pull him over. I offer to carry it for him, but he said he was fine.

He started walking down the path, and I pulled away and drove to my next destination. I immediately thought I should have stayed longer, so he made it safely to his house. But nope, I can only hope.

Btw, he also asked me if I liked his property. I said yes, it was nice. I asked if he still mows the lawn. Do you know what he said? I'm too old. Hahaha.

That's one of many stories that take place inside my car.

✱ ✱ ✱

There's a rule that we're not to pick up anyone under the age of 18. I didn't find out about this till after I had given several youths rides. Sometimes it's the parent's who order the ride. If I recognize that they're under 18, I will remind them that they'll have to get a parent or another adult to pick them up the next time. I'm sure it's for liability reasons. I've found that most youths don't mind having a conversation with a gray-haired woman as it's like talking to their grandma. One ride composed of conversations about swimming, coaster rides, rollercoasters, and traveling. Sometimes you need to be creative when the rides last more than 30 minutes.

✱ ✱ ✱

I had the cutest four-year-old girl in the car, who was chatting nonstop, saying the silliest things. Her mom and I were laughing the entire time.

* * *

A tall man climbed into the back seat. I asked if he wanted to sit up front, but he said, "No, I'm a back seat front seat driver. If you were someone I knew, I would put my head on your shoulder and do the good guy - bad guy act. But since I don't, I'll sit in the middle and make sure you don't miss my turn."

Added: oh yeah, and the smell of beer on his breath, he could have used a few breath mints.

So, the rest of the 15-minute ride was him telling me about his 34-day adventure down the Colorado River (24 days on the river). He grew up in the Salt Lake City area and loved the desert. He said the humidity in the east is just terrible and must go. (I'm thinking - good luck with that!)

Anyway - it was an interesting conversation - and I made it safely to his destination.

* * *

I dropped a girl off at her house that was painted green, and I asked if she had flowers in there? She didn't get the joke. (It wasn't that kind of a greenhouse.)

* * *

One mom flew in from Atlanta to pick up her car she had loaned to her college daughter. She previously warned her about what would happen if she allowed her friends to drive the car.

Today her daughter was losing her driving privileges. The mom was taking the car and driving back to Atlanta that afternoon.

＊ ＊ ＊

Sometimes the GPS is wrong about the location to pick up the passengers, and this tends to happen when the rider orders a ride in one spot but then walks to another one. Thankfully, the app also displays a little yellow man who represents the rider. Occasionally, this man is where the rider is, but that's not always the case.

Here is an example of such an occasion. I followed the map to the destination, but no one was around. The yellow man was on a street perpendicular to the pickup spot. I turned around and went to the next street. I pulled off to the side of the street when I saw a couple walking away from me. (I'll reference them as couple A). I opened my window and heard them arguing. He was in her face several times, calling her a b*tch. I felt bad and suddenly hoped that they weren't my riders. It didn't look like they were waiting for a ride.

But instead of canceling, I thought I'd better make sure they weren't my riders, so I drove down another street, made a U-turn, and then pulled up along the side of the road beside the girl. She was crying and wiping her face with her sleeves. I asked if she was waiting for a ride. She nodded no and waved me on.

For some reason, I wasn't ready to give up. Perhaps it was because this was going to be a long ride, and I would make more money. So, I drove to another spot and called the rider. A young man answered and said that they had gone on a walk and then gave me their new location. I double-checked my map, and after several minutes, I pulled up on the side of the road, and they each opened a door and climbed into the backseat.

I explained that I was pursuing "couple A," who was across the street, but soon discovered they weren't my riders. I added that I was glad they weren't the same couple and that I felt bad for the way the man was treating the woman.

I drove to "Couple B's" location - which ended up being a vacant lot. They put in the wrong address. The man was upset with the woman about that. The new location was an additional 16 minutes away. I offered to stop the app and, therefore, not charge for the rest of the way home (even though it was their error), but they declined and offered to buy me a meal at Bojangles. I don't think they understood that it was going to cost them more money to do that, but I didn't want to argue with them.

The woman told him it was too late for the restaurant to be open, but he insisted it was, and directed me to its location. The girl was right. I turned the car around and drove to their house.

During their conversations, the man never acknowledged the woman as being right, or even encouraging her. I felt sad and thought this relationship is not going to last long.

As the young man opened the door, the car light came on, and I turned to tell the young woman that things were going to be fine (that every couple has disagreements) and that's when I noticed that she was the same woman I had asked if she needed a ride. I reached back to hold her hand for a moment. She knew that I had figured it out. I said I would pray for her.

I learned a lesson. Don't tell every story - especially when things happen back to back.

* * *

I went on a wild goose chase that I ended up canceling after a 20-minute no-show. I went the address listed, and a prompt came up and said I wasn't where the passenger was, so I looked on the app, and the yellow man who represents the person was near a Trader Joes.

Still new to the area, I had to figure out how to get there from where I was. In the meantime, I decided to call the rider.

A woman answered yelling, "Stop calling me!"

Before I could respond, she hung up. By this time, I had reached the plaza where the yellow man was on my map. I saw a young man slip behind a building. I figured maybe that was the kid that had created the mess.

So, I think it was a prank call. Not a good way to end the night.

✱ ✱ ✱

Some passengers want to remain quiet. One day, a young woman got into the car, and I asked how her day was going.

"Terrible." She replied. And that was all she said for the next thirty minutes. When we arrived at her destination, it was behind a school building. There was a practice football field with a track, but no one was around. That's when she told me that her boyfriend ordered the ride, so she wasn't sure where he was going to meet her.

She tried to call, but he didn't answer.

I told her that I wasn't going to leave until I knew she was in a safe place. We drove back to the front of the building, and she thought she saw her boyfriend walking along the street. So I drove down and pulled up to the boys, but then she said it wasn't him. She wanted me to let her out of the car, but I said, "Let's look down this street."

There was a park across from the school that had basketball courts. As we pulled in, she saw her boyfriend walking toward her. She said he was in trouble for not giving her better directions. She left the car and slowly walked up to him. I left before they connected. I know it's not my responsibility that she gets connected with her friend, but I also don't want to feel bad if something had happened to her.

✱ ✱ ✱

I did pick up two young men at a gas station. One wore his pants at his knees but thankfully pulled them up before he got into my car. We stopped at a convenience store before heading to their destination. You could overhear one of them shout at his girlfriend (or some woman) on the phone - calling her a b*tch and hoe. (Sometimes, I get to expand my vocabulary).

* * *

One woman got into the car and asked if I knew how to get to South Park Mall. I told her that the GPS would lead me there.

She added, "if I were a professional driver, I would spend the first few weeks memorizing the city map to know where everything was so that I wouldn't make any wrong turns."

CHAPTER 18 –REASONS WHY PEOPLE USE RIDESHARE

"I was in an accident, and my car is in the shop."

✳ ✳ ✳

"I sold my car to save money. Now I don't have any car payments or a reason to spend money on oil changes, new brakes, tires, and gasoline."

✳ ✳ ✳

"I'm in from out of town, and it's easier to do rideshare than to rent a car. This way, I don't have to find the best or cheapest parking spots."

✳ ✳ ✳

"I had my license taken away from too many unpaid parking tickets."

✳ ✳ ✳

"I usually drive to work, but I needed to get some work done in the car that I can't do while I'm driving. This way, I have time for my family."

✳ ✳ ✳

"I never applied for my license. I'm scared of driving because I was in a bad car accident when I was younger. I do okay in the backseat of a rideshare car."

* * *

"I missed the bus, and it was going to be too late to wait for the next one."

* * *

"I had a flat tire and forgot that the spare was in the shop getting repaired."

* * *

"My kids overslept and missed the school bus. We don't have a car."

* * *

"The battery died, and I don't have time to wait for roadside service. I'm late for a conference."

* * *

"I bought a new car today, but since I'm going out to drink, I didn't want to risk damaging it if I was drunk coming home."

* * *

"I have a car. It stays at home because I don't have the money to pay the registration taxes. I think I'm saving money by taking a shared ride."

∗ ∗ ∗

"I was in an accident last week, but my insurance company isn't willing to pay for a rental car."

∗ ∗ ∗

"My friend lost his phone, so he can't contact me on what time he's coming to pick me up, so I ordered a ride. Though my friend works with me, so I'll be able to get a ride home."

(I wondered why they couldn't schedule a ride ahead of time. Then again, I enjoyed the ride and the pay.)

∗ ∗ ∗

"My wife and I have one car, and she needs it for her job. Usually, I carpool with friends, but today I had a meeting to attend, so I ordered a ride."

CHAPTER 19 – SEX, DRUGS, BUT NO TRICKS

One of the things I don't like about people smoking pot is that the odor of Marijuana gets into the cloth seats in my car and then lingers well after the person has departed.

Passengers have asked if I've smoked pot ever, and I tell them no, not a single time. One person asked if I've ever eaten an edible, and although I've watched characters on TV react to them, it's not something I would initiate doing, nor is it on my bucket list.

✳ ✳ ✳

When a rider asked me what I thought about LSD, I made a joke and said, "You mean Louisiana State..." Then I added, "It's not something I think about."

He asked, "Have you ever tried it?" My answer was no. Never. He said he takes it once a year to keep from getting a series of headaches. He says it makes him calmer so he can meditate and draw close to God. He added that his mom tried it when she was younger.

I responded that there were people in the 1970s that probably did try it, but I wasn't one of them.

✳ ✳ ✳

A woman riding in my car was telling me about how her family loves to go to the airport overlook to watch the planes. While there, she saw a couple get out of the front seats and then sit in the back seat of their car.

She told her boyfriend, "They're going to do it."

Sure enough, they had sex. And then the couple was arrested. You can't have sex on federal property.

* * *

Remember what it was like to sit in the back seat with your date and snuggle, hold hands, lightly kiss, etc.? Did you ever wonder what your parents thought? Surely they could hear you, even though they never tilted their head toward you.

The other night, I picked up a couple from a specialty grocery store and drove them 30-minute to their home. I would estimate that they were in their late 30s to mid-40s. I heard them whispering, but I couldn't understand what they were saying because it wasn't in English.

What I could tell, however, was how they were talking. The man's voice was high-pitched but not squeaky. When the woman said something, the man would respond as if he was a sad puppy. I'm sure his facial expressions would demonstrate - as his mouth would curl downward and his eyes would droop.

(We've all done that, right? We make the sound - mmm - one every few seconds.)

It was as if he was trying to get away with something. Or perhaps he was trying to persuade her into doing something. Soon after, I could tell that she slid over to sit closer to him (you hear these things), and she kissed him. I'm wondering – well, hoping that they're not going to continue.

Perhaps the outcome was the opening of a chip bag - as I heard the crunching of chips and the smell of something salty and a bit spicy. I was about to say - 'please pass some to me.' Actually - I wanted to say, "it's okay if you eat in my car, as long as you clean up any crumbs and don't leave trash in my car."

But I didn't say anything. I just pretended to mind my own business. After the couple left, I glanced into the backseat and saw two little chip crumbs just waiting to be tossed out. What did I do then? I turned around and kept driving.

* * *

My last passenger's husband spilled ice water in my car. I think it was wine on ice. Anyway, she cleaned it up, and he gave me a $20 tip in cash. The car had a wine scent for several days.

* * *

One night a very tipsy woman got into my car, sitting in the front seat. I don't mind people sitting there as it usually means they're open for a conversation. She thought it might be too late to go out but wanted to drive over to her favorite bar to have a shot. Just one. Unfortunately, the bar wasn't open.

We kept driving and noticing that most of the places were closed for Christmas. After driving around for a good twenty minutes, she finally suggested we stop at a gas station so she could buy a bottle of wine. While I waited in the parking lot, I glanced at the time. It was 1:45 am. I turned off my driver app so that I didn't have to give any more rides.

When I pulled into her driveway, she leaned over and gave me a little hug. Then she handed me a tip. I said thanks and then proceeded to drive the 30 minutes to my home. When I got to the next traffic light, I looked in my hand and saw a $20 bill. What a Merry Christmas that was. It's always sweet to get cash tips that I can use to buy bottles of water for the car or an occasional hamburger.

* * *

Warning: for adults only.

My last two riders got into my back seat and announced they were drunk.

"That's fine as long as you don't throw up in my car."

Then the girl asked me, "Do you mind if we have sex back here?" Uh...yes I mind. Lol.

So, the conversation continued, mostly from the girl. She says they've been best friends for years, but last night was their first time together.

I said, "it's good to wait till you know the person before having sex with them."

And then she blurted out, "Well, he's married...to my friend."

He adds, "We separated for a year. See, I can't stay with just one woman. I've had many girls over the years."

I dared to ask, "How many kids do you have?"

"Eight. Four boys and four girls all from different baby Mama's."

"You have eight baby mamas?"

"No, four. The women know each other."

"Do you pay child support?" (I'm the curious writer!)

He says, "well, I can't pay them all in the same month, but half will get some this month and half the other."

Their destination was a hotel, but first, they wanted an extra stop at a gas station. By then, we pulled into a convenience store. They're sitting in the back, not getting out. The girl says to me, "if I ask you something, will you promise not to be mad?"

"Sure, what is it?"

"Are you gay?"

"Yes."

"I told you (to him) she was. I could tell. I'm bisexual." (At this point, she is sliding closer to me and touches my shoulder briefly. I'm not worried.)

Within their conversation, he says that he doesn't like gays – he doesn't trust them. She says to me, "Do you think I should dump him because he doesn't like gays?" And although I didn't say it, I would suggest perhaps she should dump him because he has sex with more than one girl. But that's her story, not mine.

Then they get out of the car and several minutes pass, and they come back. "They didn't have the beer I like there." Stated the woman.

So, I drove them to another store that was right beside the hotel they were heading. I dropped them off and waved goodbye.

[Whew. That was an interesting ride. When they asked me earlier if their conversation bothered me, I said, "No, but to let you know, I'm a writer, but I promise not to use your names in my book."]

✳ ✳ ✳

There are some days when the riders are a little annoying. One such happening was with a woman and a man. He kept whispering to her, "Don't you love me?" He was motioning about something, so I spoke up and told them about the book I am writing and that the title is, "Do you mind if we have sex in the backseat?" To which he mumbled, "I wish that were me."

I was glad the music wasn't loud, not that I wanted to listen to their conversation, but to keep him from doing anything weird. I finally spoke up and asked if they were having sex. They said no.

It was a long, 19-min drive. I couldn't wait for the ride to end. I rated the woman three stars, which means I'll never have to give them another ride.

✳ ✳ ✳

Sometimes it doesn't bother me to work after dark unless I start watching the news. Then when I hear about the crimes at convenience stores or in dangerous neighborhoods, I want to stay home when the sun goes down. But usually, I don't give myself that option, because I know the bills don't pay themselves.

✳ ✳ ✳

Thankfully, with over 4500 rides, I hadn't run into many bad situations. Friends ask if I carry a weapon or at least some pepper spray, but I don't at this printing. I did, however, put a screwdriver inside a pocket of the driver door. I could pick it up and stab someone in the face or neck, if needed.

✳ ✳ ✳

The app doesn't tell you if you're going into a sketchy neighborhood. You learn that by listening to passengers and other drivers. One evening, while I was on my way to pick up my next passenger, a young man came up to my car as I turned the corner and asked if I could give him a ride to a bus stop. I told him I was on my way to pick up someone, but he said he had $8 cash, and it was only a few blocks away. I saw that he was carrying a big brown paper bag full of some food and a backpack. I allowed him in the car. He was probably in his late teens or early twenties. He was telling me about taking classes at the community college in town. He wanted to help people. As I dropped him off, I took only $5, and he said he was very thankful to have the other three to pay for the bus. (As far as I was concerned, that's about how much my ride would have cost him.)

So, my passenger was only a half a block away. The streetlights were dim around 10:30 pm. The app said the house was on the corner. There was a small house with a wooden fence around it and a few tall trees in the front yard. There was no porch light, and, therefore, it was impossible to see a house number. I was about to call the passenger when I heard a noise and saw a young man standing outside the car. I rolled down the window to verify who it was. The man said he had to check his backpack before getting in the car.

Then he climbed into the backseat. I asked him how his Saturday went, and he said it was fine. I started to ask him another question but noticed he had put in earplugs. I turned up the music in the front and drove to his destination. It was on the other side of town and took a good 45 minutes to drive there.

I pulled into a subdivision and found his house right away. There were curtains drawn in what must have been the living room plus a small porch light was on. As I sat in the driveway, I turned slightly toward the backseat and noticed the young man had fallen asleep. "You are home," I said loudly, but there was no movement. I left the car running and got out of the driver's side and walked around to the other side of the car and opened his door.

I tapped on his arm, "Time to wake up. You're home." Still no movement.

I walked up to the front door and rang the doorbell. No answer. I knocked on the door several times. Still no answer around 11:30 pm. I don't like to knock on doors that late, but I also didn't know what to do about the kid in the car.

I went back to the car and pulled on the boy's sweatshirt to sit him up, all the while telling him that he's at home. But then he slid back down to the seat. I thought about calling the police but decided to try something else.

As cars were pulling into the neighborhood, I waved one down. It was a woman who was delivering food to a house down the street. I told her my situation, and she said she would come back to help.

When she did, she asked me how I knew this young man. I said, "I don't. He's a passenger of mine." This woman was able to get the young man's legs out of the back seat and stood him up against the car. He woke up, and in a split second, he was pushing us away, yelling, "Get your f... hands off me."

"Hey, we're trying to help you," I responded. The young man was fidgeting to find his belongings. The woman was there to help, but he insisted he wanted to do it by himself. After grabbing his things, he stumbled to the garage and proceeded several times to press numbers in the code box, but the garage door wouldn't go up.

Suddenly, the curtains opened in the house. A woman stood there, and we started motioning her to come outside. The young man saw the woman and then walked to the front door. I followed but not directly. I wanted to make sure the boy got into the house. It was his mom. She had opened the door and then yelled at him without closing the door behind him.

The other woman told me to leave before there was any more trouble, and so I did.

On Sunday, I got a message from the rideshare company that this passenger left something in my car. I haven't gone down to look for it yet, but my suspicion was correct about him maybe having a gun with him. (He was looking for a carry case).

When we spoke on the phone, he asked if I was the one that brought him home. He said he was the crazy one. Then he asked where it was that I picked him up. He said, did you know what was going on? And I said, "Well, I saw you fumbling for something in your backpack when I picked you up, and then when I couldn't wake you when I brought you home, I figured you might have been on drugs." He didn't reply to that, so I told him that if I found his carry case, I would let him know. What I didn't tell him was that I wasn't going to return it to his house but to the rideshare driver hub in town. *I didn't find anything in my car.

✳ ✳ ✳

A man who couldn't walk in a straight line climbed into the front seat after wobbling to and fro to the car. Yes, he had too much to drink. I could tell he wasn't feeling well, but I forgot to mention to him about not throwing up in my car. Thankfully, he didn't. He did, however, thank me for driving him safely home.

* * *

Three men, most likely in their 30's, climbed into the car. The two sitting in the backseat were very talkative. It was obvious that they started early with a few beers. One of the men kept wanting me to say that this was the rowdiest ride of my day, even though it was only my fourth ride. I finally gave in and said yes, it sure would be.

* * *

There's nothing like having a passenger who shouts in the car, while his quiet friend sits in the back. The loud man got within inches of my face, where I had to put my hand up to keep him from getting any closer. He was drunk and using the "f" word a lot.

Thankfully, he wasn't mean in any way, just loud. Because I didn't feel one hundred percent safe, I gave the ride less than four stars, which means they'll never have to be in my car again. By the way, their next destination was to another bar.

* * *

I stopped at a tavern in Matthews to visit a friend who was singing in a band. I knew a few other people in the crowd, as well. A friend had texted and asked if I would take her friend home, almost an hour's drive northward. Knowing that I work for a rideshare company, her friend offered to pay me. I didn't refuse. (After the ride, I wish I had refused to take her home.)

The woman was drunk. She was so drunk that she couldn't stand up on her own and had to be led outside the bar and helped into my car. I thought about how I was going to handle her when we reached her place. She passed out in the car. I had warned her ahead of time that if she felt sick, that I would pull the car over first, and then she could open the door and throw up outside. Thankfully, we didn't have to do that.

I pulled up as close as I could to her house, which was still in the middle of the street since there were cars along the curb. I opened her door and pulled her legs out of the car and put my arms under her armpits and pulled her to her feet. She was slouched over and noncoherent. I kept talking to her, trying to make her alert enough to walk on her own, for I had no strength in myself to carry her to the door.

When we got to the first car, she immediately sat down on the hood. I was hoping that it was hers. Then I got her to stand up again and walk to the steps. I let her sit down and told her to stay there while I got the door opened. As soon as I let go, she leaned to the side and fell into a small bush. Any other day, I would have been laughing with her. Tonight, was different. It was around 1:30 am, and I was trying not to wake any neighbors. I went back and got her standing again, and she climbed the stairs and sat down in a chair on her porch. I rang the doorbell but no answer. Her daughter wasn't home. I looked in the woman's purse for her keys. Not there. I found her phone and called her daughter (the woman gave me the number), but her phone died before it went through. So, I took the phone and plugged it in my car to recharge. I used my phone to call my friend to see what I should do. She suggested putting her back into the car and bringing her to my friend's house. There was no way .I was going to be able to do that. I didn't have the strength.

Soon, I was able to call the daughter and ended up leaving a message. I went back to the woman on the porch and told her I couldn't locate her keys or her daughter and said we would have to leave. She said to look in her backpack. I looked through it but no keys. There was not a single light on the porch. Then I checked the side pockets of the bag. Yay, I found them.

I got the door opened and then helped the woman into the house and sat her down on the couch. I left one of my phone chargers and plugged in her phone. I asked if I should find something for her to throw up in if she was going to be sick. She responded that it wasn't needed.

I felt bad leaving, but she wasn't my responsibility. I left the light on and then locked her inside her home. I arrived home an hour later. She did eventually pay me for my time. I did know the woman, which is why this is in the act of kindness chapter.

* * *

We have a GPS for a reason, as it shows the fastest way to a destination. One rider who was drunk encouraged me that he knew a better way to get to his house. Everywhere he told me to turn, ended in the wrong place. Eventually, we turned into a shopping center. He apologized for giving me the wrong information. I told him it was okay, and it made the ride fun. He let me follow the map, and I got him home safely.

* * *

I pulled into a parking lot and saw two men near a tree. The young man slouched on the ground was drunk. The other man was pulling him to his feet. I was hoping they weren't my riders, but they were. The young man semi-carried his friend to the car. He opened the passenger door and stuffed his friend into the seat. He made sure his long legs were safely inside before shutting the door. Then he climbed into the back seat. His friend was unaware of what was happening.

The man apologized for his friend. They were best friends since middle school. The man in the front seat stayed in the area after high school while the other went to college in Charlotte. Now it was a few years later, and the friend came to visit, only he started drinking before the man got out of work. Then he decided to leave the apartment and continue to drink until the man got home from work.

I pulled the car into his apartment lot, and he asked if I would stay until he could get his friend settled, for he wanted to go out and drink. I said I would. He asked me again because there are drivers who do leave before the passenger returns. I stayed. It gave me time to catch on my 'Words with friends 2' games. The young man was happy to see me in the parking lot. He apologized again, and I dropped him off at a nearby pub. I asked him what he would do if his friend left the apartment again. He said he is out (asleep) for the night. Let's hope so.

* * *

Another ride put two couples in my car. They had been drinking. One asked if I was drunk, so to have some fun, I swerved the car a little. One of the women in the back said, "I love this lady. Maybe she should come to Eddie's with us." (Note: It's a good thing I'm the designated driver.)

* * *

I recognized my last rider (but not his three friends.) The last time I picked him up, he was drunk. This time was no different, but the girl said he was celebrating his 18th birthday. It makes me wonder what the drinking age is here. The ride was only $3, but he gave me a $5 tip. (The drinking age is 21).

* * *

I picked up three young men, probably around 21 years old, who was drunk. One of them had the hiccups, and they were asking me a way to get rid of them, and I gently hit the breaks to startle him, but it didn't work. I told him to hold his breath for 30 seconds. Well, then it became a times game, and he and another boy both held their breath for over a minute. And yes, the hiccups went away. Well, the two boys in the backseat - mostly one of them - was, well, drunk and saying things - f this and f that.

At one time, the other boy told him to apologize to me for something he said. (I tell you what - you can get educated in my car). Before I got them to their restaurant/bar to watch the Arizona game (oh, they're from AZ), they opened the back window and started yelling at other drivers - once saying that their tire was flat or that they dropped their wallet. I should have asked them to close the window. I was anxious to get them to their destination safely. They thanked me for the ride and said they would see me later (I just nodded my head - knowing they wouldn't!)

I picked up two women from a nightclub. I'm not sure what role they had, but we talked about prostitutes. I admitted that I've never seen women standing on the corner wearing seductive clothing in Charlotte.

"They don't dress like that. Prostitutes wear regular clothes, like jeans and tennis shoes. They're all over Charlotte. We'll look as you drive and then point them out to you."

"Seriously, that's a prostitute?" I asked when they found a young woman leaning against an old house.

"Yes. Prostitutes are housewives, secretaries, businesspeople. They're not like what you see on TV."

After dropping them off at their home, I saw the girl waiting by the house. The conversation made me more aware of my surroundings and what to watch out for in neighborhoods.

CHAPTER 20–TRANSPORTATION

From the outside of my vehicle, a person might see a sign that tells them what type of rideshare car I drive. Sometimes, I feel like the driver of other types of vehicles.

On late nights and weekends, my job is a designated driver. By being this, I keep people on and off the roads safe. Although there have been instances when I've chosen not to drive after midnight, such as on St. Patrick's Day, I'm glad there are other rideshare drivers in the area to continue to help others.

* * *

One woman was complaining about a stomachache. She said it had been bothering her for a long time. Her destination was the hospital. I approached a corner, and it had a sign for the emergency room as to the right. But I wasn't sure was that straight ahead first and then to the right or immediately to the right.

I decided to go straight first. I made the next right and then had to make another right. The woman started complaining.

"It's a good thing I'm not bleeding to death, " she stated.

"Well, I hope if you were bleeding, you would have called for an ambulance instead of from a ride-share company." I replied, "Anyway, we've arrived. Do you need a wheelchair?"

"No, I can walk in myself," she mumbled as she opened the car door and walked up to the hospital without any help.

I waited until she was inside before driving away.

* * *

I picked up a young man who worked at the airport. He wasn't feeling well. He complained of feeling feverish and asked if I had anything to drink. I gave him my water bottle. He was leaning against the door. I asked if he needed me to drop him off at the emergency room, but he stated he needed to go home first so his dad could take him. The ride to his house was about thirty minutes. I'm glad he wasn't feeling nauseated.

* * *

When I arrived at the apartment complex, a young mom and her toddler daughter got into the car. She wanted to go to the Minute Clinic at the CVS. I told her that I hoped her daughter felt better soon.

* * *

I hadn't realized that we weren't supposed to pick up school kids, even from high school, until into my third year of driving. The youngest child was around nine or ten. His dad put him in my car at his workplace, which was a gym for boxing. The drive was at least 35 minutes long. I spoke with the boy about boxing, school, and vacations.

* * *

There are a few high schools in Charlotte where I have picked up students and taken them either to their afterschool job or home. Instead of being a rideshare driver, there are days when I feel like a bus driver, even if it's just for one student.

One day, I picked up a student who had left after lunch. She said she wasn't going to miss anything that afternoon since her class had a substitute teacher. She was heading to her dad's house, where she spends half the week when she's not living with her mom.

* * *

One young man sat in the backseat holding a bunch of papers. I noticed a clear paper protector with some sheet music in it. I asked if he was taking piano lessons. He said, "No, I sing in a choir and just got promoted to Master Choir." I congratulated him. He sings bass and has been singing for years. He added that his group sings in different languages and is getting ready to perform at a local church.

* * *

I picked up a young man who was attending summer school because he had too many absences in the school year. He said it was boring and he wasn't learning anything. He did add that he understands now why it's important to go to school during the year – so you can sleep in during the summer months.

I stopped at a house in the afternoon, and two middle-school-age kids got into the car. Their destination was over twenty minutes away. The boy sat up front and was very talkative while his sister sat quietly in the back. I asked him about school and sports. I thought maybe I was taking them to their swimming lessons, but instead, I dropped them off at their gymnastics classes.

Young people can engage in conversations and your attention if you give them a chance.

* * *

One early morning, I picked up a high school student who had missed her bus. I drove down the main road and started to pull into the school lot. She informed me that this wasn't her school she was attending, even though it was in the area where she lived.

I learned that students could choose the school they want to attend based on the specialties given there. I looked at the GPS and saw where I needed to go. It was another four or so miles away. I apologized for getting her there a few minutes late.

* * *

On a late afternoon, I arrived at a high school in Union County, south of Charlotte. I picked up a substitute teacher. I told her we had something in common, for I have a degree in Elementary Education. We talked about how the students don't show respect toward teachers or subs. I shared a few occasions when students wanted me to be their teacher instead of the real teacher.

I suppose that's because I was less of a disciplinarian. As a sub, I brought candy and little toys as an incentive for good behavior. Or, as some would call it, I bribed them. This woman had retired from teaching but enjoyed being in the classroom without the extra work.

Her first stop was at a grocery store, and then I dropped her off at home. She said she had to go through the back of the house to get in. As I drove away, I thought I should have stayed longer to make sure she got in. Here's hoping she did.

* * *

A rider asked if I was a doctor. He wasn't feeling well and had already seen a paramedic earlier during his workday. It was my job to get him home. (Almost felt like an ambulance, as he felt woozy along the way. He said his blood pressure was low earlier.) Thankfully, he wasn't going home to an empty house.

* * *

One of my riders was a high school student. She said that most kids want to travel the world when they graduate, but she wants to become a child advocate lawyer.

"What grade are you in?"

"Tenth," she replied.

"Ask your school counselor for help to connect to others who can help you achieve your dream. Maybe you can do shadowing, you know, follow others at their job. Do this when you're in high school, and even those people will encourage you and point you in the right direction."

She thanked me for the advice, and I'm confident she will succeed.

* * *

One of my riders was a senior in high school. The student dressed in black pants and a white shirt and tie. He was presenting his senior project today. I tried to get him to practice it for me, but he was too shy.

* * *

Although I've never felt like a fire engine while driving, I was, in a sense, chased by one at the airport. I arrived at the airport only to find long lines for arrivals, extending a quarter of a mile away from the terminal. I chose the middle lane, for that's the one that taxi drivers and other rideshare drivers use to approach their customers.

Ten minutes into the wait, I hear a siren. I look in the rearview mirror and then side mirrors and see a fire engine trying to make its way toward the terminal. So,

I moved my car to the right lane to get out of its way.

The fire engine appears directly behind me in that lane. So I move into a small road off to my right. Sure enough, that's where the engine wants to turn. The horn was deafening. I moved my car as far up the lane and then

had to turn to the right. The fire engine had turned and then gone straight ahead toward the runway. I was now out of line.

I called my passenger to explain my delay and told her I was sorry, but I would be another 10 – 15 minutes. I felt bad when I finally reached her and found out that she was pregnant, about seven months along, and was tired of standing by the time I picked her up. There was no conversation taking place in my car on that trip.

CHAPTER 21 –U-TURNS AND ONE-WAY STREETS

I was in the left lane on a four-lane divided road waiting to enter the turning lane, and the line of cars was barely moving. I couldn't believe how long it was taking. A few cars ahead slid into the right lane.

Finally, I decided to take my chances. Once I passed a few cars, I could slip back into the left lane. I drove past three cars and a box truck and then found the left lane empty. Because the truck was tall, you couldn't tell it was blocking the road.

* * *

One too many rides. I picked up three guys in uptown near Independent Square. There were cars everywhere and so I decided to make a U-turn. I realized I didn't leave myself enough space when we heard a crack coming from the front of my car. It hit the curb hard.

The young man announced that he wasn't paying for the damage. I told him I wouldn't charge him for it. It was my fault. Then I drove about seven miles to their destination before looking at any damage.

I stopped at a nearby gas station only to find the front grill and bumper unhinged from the car. I snapped in what I could. I was glad it didn't fall off while I was driving.

* * *

While waiting in a specific lot for rideshare drivers, I was pinged to pick up a man who lived close to the golf course. I drove in his direction, knowing full well that I would be asked to turn around. I had to make a U-turn. I called the person and explained why I couldn't pick him up.

His options were to walk to the clubhouse and get on the bus that brought him to the pickup lot or stay home. I felt bad. Many others who lived in that neighborhood couldn't leave. Fortunately, others had a vehicle with a special pass. This man had neither of those.

✳ ✳ ✳

After picking up two girls at a restaurant, we were halfway to their hotel when she received a phone call that someone had found her wallet on the table. The girl explained she made sure to grab her umbrella; she didn't even think about the other. I made a U-turn back to the restaurant. It didn't take her long, and we were soon on our way to the hotel.

✳ ✳ ✳

There were two times when passengers forgot something at their home, and I had to turn the car around. One of them was with a young woman who was going to a concert at the Music Factory.

We were within a mile of the drop-off spot, and she started looking for her tickets and realized she had left them at home. I made a U-turn, drove 20 minutes back to her house, and a few minutes later, we were on our way back to the venue. She was grateful.

The other one was a man who was going to the baseball game. Again, we were close to the venue when he realized he forgot his wallet. He was sorry for having me turn around, but I don't mind going back. More time on the road is more money in my pocket.

✳ ✳ ✳

My rider destination took me to the University of North Carolina campus, outside of Charlotte. I followed the GPS on my phone. It led me to a brick pathway, the width of a single lane road. It was a Sunday afternoon, and there didn't seem to be very many students out and about. I sat in my car, wondering if cars were on this road.

I saw a campus truck parked off to the side up the road away but no moving vehicles. I didn't find another way to get to my passenger without driving on it. I decided to take the chance. I drove up to the intersection and then turned left.

Several groups of students walked by, giving me a concerned glance, but no one stopped to tell me otherwise. When another group walked past, I rolled down my window and asked, "Am I allowed to drive on this road?"

"No," he laughed.

And to that, I backed up to a place where I could turn around and then retraced my steps back to the parking lot. I called the rider, and he met me there. He also laughed when I told him what I had done.

I said, "Leave it to the gray-haired grandma to drive on campus where you're not supposed to drive."

Always give a warning to the passengers when doing a U-turn on a two or undivided four-lane road. The last thing you want is for a passenger to fall over in the backseat because you whipped around the corner too fast. That's not a good way to get a tip.

CHAPTER 22 –VACATIONS, THE DREAM KIND

One popular question I love to ask is, "If you could go anywhere in the world on a dream vacation, and money was no problem, where would you go? The answers varied, but they usually started with, "That's a really good question."

∗ ∗ ∗

I had a conversation with a passenger the other day. She admitted she works all the time and has never even thought about that question. I told her it's okay to dream. You never know what the future brings.

Several stated they wanted to go to Europe or even a European Cruise so you could see many of the countries along the coast. Others said Hawaii or Alaska. One even said, South Africa. Another said, "Anywhere hot!"

∗ ∗ ∗

Here are some places people suggested for a dream vacation: Thailand, Bora Bora, Hawaii, Bahamas, Dubai, Mumbai, Barcelona, Iceland, Ireland, Africa, Alaska, Mediterranean, and even Myrtle Beach.

∗ ∗ ∗

The idea is not to ask someone who returned from a two-week vacation. Their answer was, "I want to stay home."

The question often turns back to me. My dream vacation is to visit Prince Edward Island because that's where the story "Anne of Green Gables" was filmed. Plus, I want to go to Nova Scotia and drive along the rocky shoreline. Then I'll travel across Canada to Vancouver and visit Jamestown to see the setting for the show "When Calls the Heart."

* * *

Several of the interesting rides were conversations about where they would go on a dream vacation. Several chose Italy. But if it was all expenses paid, then it was to Australia, New Zealand, or Africa.

My response was to Nova Scotia and Prince Edward Island. One passenger said, "we didn't think of that. We'll have to add it to our list."

* * *

CHAPTER 23 – WHAT DO WE HAVE TO DO TO GET IN THIS BOOK?

One rider asked if he mooned the car behind us - would he get in this book? I said, sure. But he didn't do it. I put him in here anyway.

* * *

A woman clammed up when she heard I was writing a book. Her husband was sitting in the front seat while she was lying down in the back.

Every time her husband opened his mouth to answer a question I had asked, she told him to shush. Finally, I shared with him some of the crazy stories I was writing in it. When I arrived at their home, the man apologized for his inebriated wife.

* * *

A couple got in my car for a ride home from dinner. I told them about this book I was writing, and they asked how they could get in it. I asked if they've done any good deeds or acts of kindness, and the husband told me that his wife volunteered for a mission in the West Virginia mountains to help with the low-income families. I said, "Well, there you go."

* * *

One young man who was drunk when I picked him up was also very kind and respectful. His destination was to a convenience store and then back home. He was house-sitting for his parents. He shared how he spent time in the army before getting injured and returning home.

He also spent time as a rideshare driver. We shared stories. I told him about my longest ride and how I didn't receive a tip. He reached into his pocket and pulled out some cash and gave me $6. I tried to give it back, but he was persistent. It's nice to know people appreciate what you do.

* * *

Many people found a place in this book, some who had no idea of its existence. This chapter has few entries as there are not many who followed through with doing anything worth writing about to receive recognition.

One passenger shared his grumpy self for the entire 18-minute ride. From the moment of the phone call to verify his pickup spot to the moment, he closed the door at his destination. It's easy to recognize sad people. The best thing to do is not to engage with them.

Thankfully, there was another passenger in the car who was willing to have a quiet, peaceful conversation, despite the self-absorbed man sitting next to him.

The talkative rider worked as a painter for both residential and commercial buildings. The company he works with is called Action Jackson Home Services, in the Carolinas. He explained how real estate investors are wary about hiring painters who scam the investors by charging them twice for the service. These scammers know that the investor is more likely to pay the second bill instead of waiting months for the court to rule in their favor, which also adds monthly maintenance costs in the real estate.

His painting company does not participate in these scams.

* * *

Another couple was interested in this book but didn't have anything to add except that they probably won't be in it. But I said, "well, you did ask about it. That's something."

* * *

As I'm finishing this book, I mention it to my riders. One young man who got in the car for a 37-minute ride shared how he used to be a driver. We talked about common questions riders would ask, such as "What else do you do? Or "What's your craziest ride?"

After I recited the chapter titles, he said he didn't think he had any content for it. Then he said, "If you come back at 3 am to take me home, you'll find a different person, and then maybe I could give you something to write in the book."

I told him I wasn't staying out till 3 am so he said he would be done at 2:30 am. He promised he wouldn't take his clothes off, and I said, "Darn."

[He was referring to a story I told him about another new driver. In his first week, there was a woman who got into the front seat of his car and proceeded to take off her clothes, all the way to her underwear. He was saying things like, "What are you doing? I'm married." But she was drunk. So, he called the last number on her phone, and that person met him, and together they got the drunk woman home.]

* * *

One rider was a young man who taught middle-school kids. The first thing he asked after entering the car was, "Are you a smoker?"

"No, I can honestly say, I've never tried it."

"Yes, I think you have. But not cigarettes. It smells like you've been smoking pot."

"Well, it wasn't me. It must have been another rider." I was getting irritated. Finally, he stopped teasing me.

The man was a middle school teacher. I told him it takes people with a purposeful heart to teach young adults as they're experiencing the mental and physical changes happening in their bodies.

After sharing about my fiction books, he agreed that it was something young people who also identify as LGBTQ need.

In this case, being an LGBTQ ally, I put his conversation in the book.

CHAPTER 24 – EXPERIENCES AS A DRIVER

The passenger is always right, even if they're sometimes wrong. I was following the GPS to a yoga place, and it was leading me around to the back entrance.

Previously, the rider told me that she was running late, so when I didn't turn where she expected, she asked me to stop the car and let her out there. So, I did. I could have got her to the destination faster if she stayed in the car.

* * *

While transporting a passenger to her destination, a younger woman flagged me down as I turned the corner onto a side street. She was walking in front of a truck that was idling there. The woman appeared frantic. I rolled down my window, and she asked if I could help her.

She worried about her mom, who went to a hospital due to having a heart attack. I motioned her toward the passenger front seat. She turned back toward the truck and told that driver to go ahead. (I don't know if he had stopped or if perhaps, she had gotten out of his truck to come into my car.)

My passenger shared with the girl that she worked at the same hospital and wondered where her mom was now, and the girl said the fifth floor. My passenger responded that she worked that floor also but was a housekeeper and asked for the mom's name. But to my memory, she never told us. And, I don't recall her telling me her name either.

I dropped my passenger off. The girl seemed anxious. She said, "I've never asked anyone for anything before; I'm so embarrassed." I told

her that I have six kids in other cities, and sometimes they need to
rely on others to help them when I can't be there. I asked her what
she needed. She said, "I don't want to ask you for anything."

But I said (later I realized this is where I should have started
questioning her) "Just tell me what you want, and I'll do my best to
help you." I should have told her that I was almost broke myself and
didn't have much to give her. But I felt like God put her on my path for
a reason and that I should trust that everything would work out.

She said she needed $47 for gas because the floater in the gas
gauge broke in her car. Someone was waiting with a can of gas for
her but wouldn't put it in without the cash. Plus, she needed to get her
11-year-old brother some food. Finally, she added that she needed a
phone because hers was run over by another car that morning.

She asked if I knew where a Metro PCS was, and I said no. I let her
use my phone to Google places nearby. We stopped at an AT&T
store, but after entering and seeing several others who needed help,
she changed her mind and decided to go to the Walgreen's instead.

I seriously didn't have any money to spend but felt like whatever I
gave her; I would have to keep driving that night until I paid myself
back. I didn't want to buy her a phone unless it was like a cheaper flip
phone.

I dropped her off at Walgreen's and went to the park, and she turned
and said, "Don't leave me," and I was like, "No, that's not the kind of
person I am."

In the store, she tossed a couple of sundresses on the counter and
grabbed some wet wipes and a travel kit – a man's razor kit. I
happened to notice it in the car. They didn't sell phones there.

She also grabbed a bottle of water (I was thinking 'what about one for
me?') and one other item. She was on her period, and so perhaps she
got some protection. Anyway, they rang it up, and I slid in my credit
card. After spending $46, I sat in the car wondering why in the world I
just bought all that stuff for a girl who supposedly was only looking for
a phone.

She suddenly said, "I'd better get back to my brother. What bank do you have to go to?" I said, "Any bank," so she directed me to the 7-11, which has an ATM inside. She had asked for $47 for gas and some extra money to buy herself a phone for her trip back to Wilmington, North Carolina – about a four-hour drive.

On the way, she changed her dress while sitting on the passenger side. She said something about not wanting the social worker to see the bloodstain on her dress (from having her period). Yet I had to clean a small bloodstain spot on the seat.

When I arrived at the gas station, I swiped my credit card, but I didn't have the right PIN. It had been a while since I used it. I thought about the $83 I had in my checking. I figured God would provide it, so I got $80 out of the ATM and handed it to her in the car. I told her that was all I could give her. She said, thanks.

I was about to turn toward the McDonald's when she redirected me down a side street. We passed a police car, and then I pulled the car over to the curb. She grabbed her belongings (or where they mine?) and stood there as I drove off.

I remembered that I forgot to give her my address so she could mail the money back to me but then figured that I was probably just taken as a fool and would never see her or the money again.

I started to think about all the red flags in her story – and wondered why I allowed her to take advantage of me in the first place.

First off, I should not have allowed her in my car – especially since I had a passenger in there. What is wrong with me? Why do I have trouble standing up for myself and my safety? Don't worry – I was given lectures about this from several different people – all with their best interest in my safety.

I drove back to that neighborhood the next day – just thought I'd look around, but it's one of those neighborhoods where driving slow could make you look like a drug dealer, so I just kept going and then scooted out safely. Some day, I'll quit wearing my heart on my sleeve, and be strong and firm while telling people, No!

* * *

The rideshare app tends to freeze, even in the middle of a ride. I was
pinged to pick up a rider, but then the app froze to the point that I
didn't even know the address of where I was supposed to go.

The GPS led me to a street (when it was still working), but I didn't
have a house number. Eventually, the rider canceled the trip. I had to
turn my phone completely off and then on again for it to start working.

* * *

My destination was a bar. As I pulled up to the establishment, I
noticed a man setting half glass of beer down on a table as he and
another young man walked toward my car. My initial thought was for
them to keep walking, but they stopped and got inside. We exchanged
names, making sure they were in the correct car.

One announced right away that he was drunk. I asked if he felt sick,
for the last thing I wanted was for someone to throw up in my car. He
said he was fine. But as I pulled out of the parking lot, I accidently hit
a pothole, and the car swayed a bit. (I thought - he might be sick
now).

The ride was going to be 25-minutes away, which gave us plenty of
time to talk. One of the boys requested stopping at a Cook-Out
restaurant on the way. The drunk man was very rude to the cashier by
saying crude and vulgar words.

Since he was sitting behind me, he was the one who had to hand over
the money and then receive the food when we pulled up to the
window. Before we reached the window, I asked him to be respectful
towards the server. His brother agreed. But he wouldn't listen. He
continued to tease the cashier by holding tightly onto the bills so she
couldn't take them, and then when he let them go, he briefly grabbed
her hand. I was embarrassed. I hoped that the cashier didn't think I
was their mother.

Thankfully, they didn't start eating in the car. But as we were driving along a curvy road, I suddenly felt two hands on my shoulders, as if being attacked from behind. He didn't squeeze them or hurt me. I was just surprised. He mumbled something about wanting to kill me, and his brother told him to settle down and quit acting weird.

A few miles from the house, they were asking me what I thought about pot - and I gave them a response. And that same young man invited me into their house to meet their other brother who would love to talk politics with me. Um, no, thanks.

I gladly let them out of my car and went on to pick up my next rider, who was 10 minutes away. When I got within six, the sober young man called me (I answered on his phone, which I found on the floor behind me, plugged into the charger). He wanted me to return it right away for $20. I told him I'd have to call the next rider first, and then I would return it.

The next rider decided to wait me out and not cancel the ride, thankfully. I turned around and headed back. Now, where was that turn? When you're following an app at night, it's hard to notice details such as the names of roads.

After a few minutes, I called him back to get his address. Five minutes later, I pulled in the driveway, and the young man met me at the car and thanked me. He said he'd leave a tip on the app. "$20, right?" He asked if we agreed on that – Yes, I said. He took his phone, and I was finally able to leave and go to my next rider. By the way, he didn't leave a tip.

* * *

Stopping at a local brewery, one young man sits in the front seat, and four others climb into the backseat. I say, "I can only take four people." But they said they were skinny and could fit. Plus, the other two in the bachelor party left, and they didn't want to pay for two cars. I agreed to let the fifth one squeeze in though I could have refused them. The bachelor was home sleeping, and his brother had to leave the bar for being too rowdy and getting sick. These five men were from out of town, so I dropped them off in an area with plenty of food, beer, and entertainment.

* * *

One of the saddest rides. I picked up a girl at her work after several wrong turns (my GPS map was wrong; it led me to a dead-end).

The girl was on her phone, talking to her boyfriend. She was saying something like, "You can figure out how to get to the store, but you can't figure out how to fix our relationship." He was dumping her. For much of the 20 minutes ride to her home, she cried. I felt bad but didn't have any words of wisdom.

She asked to stop at the gas station before arriving at her house, and I did. I told her I was sorry about her situation and wondered if she was getting some chocolate or perhaps some wine. She thanked me for the concern. She didn't tell me what she got.

As I was dropping her off at home, I told her she had my permission to beat the stuffing out of her pillow. (Of course, she doesn't need permission to do that. It was the only thing I could think to say.)

I wanted to tell her to remember she was worthy, and she doesn't need a man to give her value, but again, I only knew her by her first name and from where I picked her up.

* * *

Life is hard. Earlier I had a young mom (widow) with a 5-year-old son (he was not in the car). We were talking about grief, and I reminded her that the second year is sometimes harder than the first (she was in her tenth month). I said you should let the tears flow whenever they come.

I am blessed with this job, for I feel it's such a small world with so much in common with others. I'm glad I can talk to my passengers.

* * *

There are times when you need to put the other person ahead of your gain. My first ping took me to a house. After waiting a few minutes, I glanced at the map to see where the destination was and realized it was a two-stop ride. The first stop was 13 miles away and then back to the house.

There was a problem. The rider was already at the first stop. So, I called and explained that it would get the home faster if they canceled the ride and ordered a new one. But they felt like they would lose their money if they canceled. I tried to explain that if I drove to them and then back, it would charge them the amount they didn't want to pay. But I was expected to come.

So, I selected "picked up" and proceeded to drive to their destination. When the woman and her daughter got in the car, they further explained that the first driver dropped them off and then drove away, leaving them behind.

So, knowing she already paid for two trips (one for them getting there and one for me), I stopped the app and took her back to her house for free.

CHAPTER 25 – WHY NOT SHARE THIS TOO

I met this nice young man who called himself a homeboy. As I was telling him about my car, he said it was 'dope.'

And I was like, "What?"

He said, "'Dope,' you know, nice."

"Oh," I responded, "I didn't know about that meaning."

Then as I was telling him more about some other things, and he interrupted and said, "facts."

Again, I was baffled.

He said, "That's what you say when someone is giving you true information, you say 'facts.' Now, how would you say it?"

I responded with a smile, "Facts."

"Yeah, that was 'dope,'" he said.

And there it was, my first lesson is 'homeboy language,' or so I thought. That's a generational language, as a friend from church taught me the word, 'shade,' meaning to turn your eyes away from someone. I have a lot left to learn.

There have been a few times when the app stopped working in the middle of a job. One time, I had picked up a young man and his father at the airport. When I arrived in Zone D (arrival section for rideshare riders), the app froze. It wouldn't let me confirm on picking him up. Thankfully, my passengers agreed to give me directions instead of spending uninterrupted time chatting in the backseat. At one point, I thought it was working, but it kept directing me back to the airport to pick him up, even though he was already in my car. It was very frustrating.

The young man started worrying that I wasn't going to receive money for this trip. He said to me, "I know you're not a stripper, but I'm going to pay you with ones."

I laughed as it was the first time someone has said that to me. And now that I think about it – how does the rider know I'm not a stripper? Has he met all of them? LOL. Thankfully, by the time we reached his home, the app was back on-line, and his payment was received so that he could keep his ones.

* * *

I love it when the passengers want to engage in a conversation though there have been some instances when talking was not on the agenda. One gentleman got in my car, and my first question to him was, "How was your flight?"

He responds, "I don't want to talk about it."

What do you say after that? I relayed a story about a friend of mine who had lost luggage and had airlines detour him across the country, and the passenger said he understood that.

Then he said, "If you don't mind, I'm going to sit back here and sulk all the way home. I'd appreciate it if you didn't talk to me."

And so, I didn't. It was a forty-minute ride. I pulled into the neighborhood and was about to stop at a house, and he looks up and says, "This isn't my neighborhood."

Oh boy, he was having a bad day. I felt terrible, but what was I to do. He found the correct address was another fifteen minutes away. When he finally left the car, he said, "Thanks for letting me sulk." He left me a tip.

* * *

With plenty of good people in the world, it is worth the risk to share your experiences with others because that is how you learn. When those involved are receptive to having a conversation, we can begin to grow more comfortable with one another. Remember, each person has their own unique beliefs, and even some of our external differences are not always apparent either.

* * *

A young woman had two grocery carts full of everything from blinds to bananas to water bottles. She had moved into a house with two or three others and was having fun at Walmart picking out things to furnish it.

Thankfully, her roommates were home when I backed the car into their driveway. I helped where I could and left things on the front porch. It took them several trips to the car for the backseat, and the trunk was also full of things.

* * *

A woman told me that she lost over 200 pounds when she had her gall bladder removed. She became a vegan and a hula-hooper for exercise. I have no desire to become a vegan, but I'd love to try exercising with a hula hoop.

* * *

One of my riders asked which one I preferred, long or short rides. I said that longer rides bring in more money, but shorter ones help me meet more people. And this was a short ride but long enough for him to tell me that he was an ice skate instructor who encouraged me to get back on the ice. I wanted to laugh out loud but held it in. I told him I don't have the balance for that anymore.

* * *

I get overly excited when I meet people who love to read young adult fiction because then I tell them about my book series titled, "You'll Always Be Close to My Heart." Sure enough, several have ordered them through Amazon.

* * *

One rider stated he was heading to basic training in a few months. He set personal goals such as, get a dealer's license for selling cars, earn a degree in mechanical engineering with a double minor in computer science and drafting. He also wants to start a nonprofit to help young kids know how to dress for different occasions. He says he loves wearing a bow tie when he's not playing basketball. This young man has plenty of ambition. I'm sure he'll accomplish his goals.

* * *

I met a reviewer (for this book) when I picked up a young woman who teaches at a Christian school. Something was happening in the neighborhood that caused the school to go on lockdown. This woman was able to sneak out before the doors locked.

After we left the area, I told her about writing this book. She was curious about how I decided on the title. She laughed as I shared the story. She mentioned that I didn't seem to be shocked by their request. I suppose you learn to let things go and not expect the worst in people. Though I know the worst does happen at times.

As she was leaving the car, she mentioned about checking the book out when it was published. That's when I asked if she wanted to be a reviewer. She jumped at the chance.

I picked up a young teen boy who put his skateboard in the trunk and then sat down in the backseat. He told me he was in the ninth grade. I asked him if he thought at all about what he wants to do after he graduates.

"I want to become a veterinarian. Right now, I have two dogs, a rabbit, and a pet snake that's about four and a half feet long. My parents don't go into my room because they don't like snakes."

I joked with him that it was a good thing because then he didn't have to worry about his mom coming in to clean his room.

"We order frozen rats to feed the snake every week. Then after the snake eats one, I can't pick it up for 2-3 days, or it will vomit up the food. After the first day, you can see the shape of the rat body in the snake's body. It's weird to see, but that's how it eats it. The snake grows only 2-3 inches a year but will grow up to 7-8 ft long. I keep it in an aquarium, but sometimes when mom's not home, I'll bring it out and let it roam my room. One time I couldn't find it. I looked everywhere but couldn't find it. That's pretty much when Mom decided not to go into my room again. Then later, I reached under my bed to grab a notebook out of a box, and there he was."

"I knew a young man in Pennsylvania that went to schools and churches to teach kids about reptiles. Maybe you could do something similar in places here, such as helping them identify between poisonous and non-poisonous snakes. Even adults need repetitive lessons." He said he would look into it.

* * *

A passenger shared a situation about another driver who pulled the car over to the side of the road. He got out and walked around the car so he could urinate. He apologized when he got back into the car. My thought is that it pays to be a man. There have been many times when I've had to drive uncomfortably – waiting for the time to go off-line and find a restroom.

* * *

A young woman was in the fourth generation of the family who resided in Rock Hill SC. Her father was responsible for putting the Christmas lights on the tops of all the buildings in town, including the infamous Santa Claus and his sleigh. As she was exiting the car, I told her to give a big thanks to her dad for all his hard work.

* * *

Whatever you do, don't encourage your passengers to leave the car while it's moving. Wait until the traffic has stopped, as well.

* * *

Gross. Disgusting. Sticky floors. There were urine stains everywhere on the toilet, the floor, and the wall. The last guy didn't even flush. The women's door wouldn't open, so I had to use the men's bathroom at a 7-eleven. Ironically there was a sign on the door about keeping the free bathrooms clean. I almost laughed out loud! Besides the toilet, the sink and floor were dirty. I'm surprised I got out of there before cleaning it all up - with only the toilet paper.

CHAPTER 26 – ZOMBIES, ZEALOUS, AND ZANY

My driving, or should I say, my car helps people fall asleep during the ride. One woman fell asleep, and it was hard to wake up when we arrived at her house. I thought about pulling into the driveway but stayed on the street. I called her name several times and touched her shoulder to awaken her. Then when she finally got out of the car, she started going across the street. I thought she was walking away from her house.

As she went into the house, I realized she had put the wrong number in the address. I made sure she was safely inside before driving away.

$$* \quad * \quad *$$

There are parties all over the city for this All-Star event. I heard Shaq is in town, as is Will Smith. I would love to catch a glimpse of them someday.

$$* \quad * \quad *$$

A passenger was quiet in the backseat after spending time on the phone with his spouse. They were speaking in another language. I hate it when they do that, I can't eavesdrop and then add to the conversation. LOL. When we were about four miles from his house, I asked if he needed to stop and get anything from the convenience store. I was thinking, maybe a bottle of wine or a nice rose for his wife.

There was no response. I couldn't turn my head around but imagined why he might be so quiet. Did he die? Then a few minutes later, I heard him snore. My driving had put him to sleep. That was a good thing; otherwise, I wasn't sure what to do with his body, had he died. He woke up when we went over the speed bumps in his neighborhood. I didn't even acknowledge the fact that he had fallen asleep. He got out, grabbed his bags, and walked to his house.

✳ ✳ ✳

I had the privilege to go on a Justin Bieber hunt. Was I a stalker? No. There was a young woman from France who was attending the PGA Golf tournament and spotted Justin Bieber there. She needed to talk to him, but every time she came close, he was busy chatting with someone else.

Just when she thought she had him cornered, she turned to find him gone. That's where I come in. I picked her up at the rideshare lot. She said that if she were in France, she would know where he was staying. She needed to speak with him, and therefore, we needed to find him. I asked where she wanted to look first, and she said the airport.

So, on the way, I mentioned that the airport was small, at least in the area before security. Surely if he were on his way there, he would be past security before we arrived. I asked if she knew him personally, and she said no.

I told her that I was proud of her because some people who have a goal in mind don't always follow through when they realize they'll probably fail. But she was determined to look at the airport even though he was most likely not there. I reminded her to go down to Zone-D when she stopped looking, so she could order another rideshare back to her hotel.

By the way, one of the passengers the following day said they saw Justin Bieber at the golf tournament that day.

* * *

One rider asked me to go with his group to the party (reception) and have a shot, which I kindly rejected. But the very next rider was heading to the same bar, so I told him to look for the guy and tell him, "Sue said I could have her shot." Ha-ha.

* * *

A passenger told me about a dance called Krump. "According to Wikipedia, Krump is a street dance popularized in the United States, characterized by free, expressive, exaggerated, and highly energetic movement. The youths who started Krump saw the dance as a way for them to escape gang life and "to express raw emotions in a powerful but non-violent way." Thankful to hear about this activity.

* * *

One young man who works at a fast-food restaurant said a woman wanted extra lettuce on her sandwich. So, he put more on it.

As he handed it to her, she said, "Do you think I'm stupid? I want more lettuce than that!"

To which the young man replied, "You could have all the lettuce you want, but it won't help you lose any weight."

I laughed and then asked if he got fired when he said that.

He said, "No, they just put me in the kitchen away from the customers. By the way, the woman should have ordered a salad."

There have been a few instances when the GPS has led me in the wrong direction, thereby getting the passengers to their destination a few minutes late. My standard reply is, "Tell your boss that a gray-haired lady was driving and missed a turn." Of course, sometimes we can blame it on the traffic or the restricted one-way roads in uptown Charlotte.

❋ ❋ ❋

My last rider was a young mom, and we picked up two kids at daycare and brought them back home. She didn't even put a seatbelt on the three-year-old, and only on the one-year-old after watching a truck dodge out in traffic. Anyway, the boy gets in the car and then asks me if I have a baby in my stomach. Lol. I said I wish I had that excuse.

❋ ❋ ❋

I had a fun couple in my car. They've been dating for three months. She said that on their first date, she ordered nachos before he arrived. She decided she was going to have a good night - with or without him. He did show up on time (she was early).

I mentioned bacon roses, and now they're going to figure out how to make them. I told the man as he got out of the car, that he might be guaranteed six months if he gave her those.

CHAPTER 27 - APPENDIX

Here is an alphabetical list of the different COUNTRIES where the passengers live (or were born). Is your country here?

A – Argentina, Austria, Australia

B –Bangladesh, Brazil,

C – Chile, China, Colombia, Costa Rica

D – Denmark

E – Ecuador, Eritrea

F - France

G – Germany, Ghana, Greece, Grenada

H – Honduras

I – Iceland, India, Ireland, Italy

J – Japan

K –

L –

M –Madagascar, Mexico

N – Norway

O – Ontario (Canada)

P –Peru, Philippines, Portugal

Q – Qatar

R –Russia

S – Saskatchewan, Saudi Arabia, South Africa, South Korea, Spain, Switzerland

T – Thailand, Turkey

U – Uganda, United Arab Emirates, United Kingdom, United States

V – Venezuela, Vietnam

W –

X -

Y –

Z -

Here is an alphabetical list of the different OCCUPATIONS the passengers in my rideshare car do. Is your occupation here?

.

A – Accountants, actors, actuary, advertising specialist, aged care worker, airline ground crew, artist, author, auto detailer

B – Baker, ballet dancer, bank worker, bar attendant, beautician, body artist (tattooist), bookkeeper, bouncers, brewer, builders, bus driver

C – Café manager, call center, career counselor, chef, chemical engineer, chemist, childcare manager, cinema worker, clinical psychologist, commercial housekeeper (hotels), conference organizer, cook, customer service manager

D – Dancer, delivery driver, dental hygienist, developer programmer, domestic engineer

E – Early childhood teacher, electrician, entertainers, entrepreneurs

F – Fashion designer, fast-food cooks, film & video producers, financial planner, fitness instructions, flight attendants, forklift driver

G – Game developer, graphic designer, groomer (dog), ground crew,

H – Hairdresser, home health aide, hospice social worker, human resources support

I –Intensive care specialist, interior designer

J – Janitor, jewelry designer, job coach, journalist,

K – Kennel assistant, kitchen staff,

L – Late-night shift staff, laundry worker, lawyer, librarian

M – Makeup artist, marketing specialist, massage therapist, mechanical engineer, medical diagnostic radiographer, medical oncologist, midwife, minister of religion, model, motor mechanic, musician, music therapy

N – Nanny (au pair), network administrator, nurse practitioner, nursing support worker, nutritionist

O – Obstetrics, occupational therapist, office manager

P – Parking lot attendants, pastry cook/chef, patient care assistant, personal assistant, pharmacy technician, postal deliver officer, primary school teacher, prop & scenery, maker

Q – Quality control officer, quality team leader

R – Radio presenter, a realtor, receptionist, a registered nurse, restaurant manager

S – Sales assistant, sailor, secondary school teacher, security engineer, ship crewman, social worker, special needs, sports coach, strippers (go-go girls), students, substitute teacher, systems analyst

T –Teachers, teacher's aide, ticket collector/usher, tour guide, tourist information officer, train workman, transportation coordinator, travel consultant, truck driver, TV show host

U –Underwriter, university lecturer

V – Video editor, visual arts & crafts professional

W – Waiter, welfare worker, winemaker,

X –eXtras (actors),

Y – Yoga instructor, youth worker

Z – Zoning Administrator, (I'd love to add a zookeeper, but Charlotte doesn't have a zoo.)

✳ ✳ ✳

Restaurants and Breweries (B) in Charlotte

Passengers ask for recommendations. These are places where I'm picking up or dropping off people.

A – Alexander Michael's (a tavern in the Historical 4th ward), Aria Tuscan Grill, Azteca Mexican,

B – Bad Daddy's Burger Bar, Birdsong (B), Bricktops,

C – Cantina 110, Cava, Capital Grille, Catawba (B), Chima Brazillian Steakhouse (serving all you can eat meat and veggie skewers; Michael Jordan owns the 7th floor.),

D – Dressler's,

E – Eddies Place, Enat Ethiopian,

F – Fig Tree, 5Church, Fahrenheit (Upscale rooftop restaurant), Fiamma, Fitzgerald's (a bar featuring the Pittsburgh Steeler's memorabilia), Free Range (B), French Quarter,

G – Gallery,

H – Haberdish, Heist (B), Hoppin (B),

I – Ink N Ivy,

J – JJ's Red Hots,

K – Kid Cashew, King's Kitchen,

L – Landmark, Lang Van Vietnamese, Legion (B), Lenny Boy (B), Lucky Dog Park (B), Luce,

M – McNinch House, Merchant, and Trade (rooftop restaurant), Mert's Heart and Soul (Southern cooking), Midnight Diner, Midwood Steakhouse, Miro Spanish Grill,

N – Napa on Providence, NoDa (B),

O – 131 Main, Olde Mecklenberg (B), Open Kitchen,

P –Paco's Tacos, Palm Charlotte, Pinky's Westside Grill, Pho Hoa Noodle Soup, Price's Chicken Coop, Portofinos Italian, Protagonist (B),

Q –Queen City Q, Q Shack,

R – Red Clay Ciderworks (B), Red Rocks Café, Resident Culture (B), Roosters Wood-fire Kitchen,

S – Sabor Latin Street Grill, Soho Bistro, Southbound, Southern Tier (B), Suffolk Punch (B), Sugar Creek (B), Sullivan's steakhouse, Sycamore, (B)

T – 300East, Triple C (B), Tupelo Honey, Tea Room,

U –Unknown (B), Upstream,

V –VBGB Beer Hall (B),

W – Wan-Fu Chinese, Wooden Robot (B)

X, Y, Z –

CHAPTER 28 TIPS FOR RIDERS

- Be respectful to the driver and other passengers
- When possible, leave a note on the app for your driver at your exact location, especially at the airport.
- When waiting to be picked up, don't stand exactly on a street corner. Stand, a minimum of a cars' length away, to give the driver room to stop.
- Wear your seatbelt
- Ask the driver if it's okay to eat or drink. If yes, don't leave a mess.
- Be considerate and leave a tip.
- If you have a dog, but not a service dog, call your driver ahead of time to ask if they mind if the dog comes in the car. Then leave a tip for the dog.
- Abide by the state law of "no opened containers of beer, wine, or other alcohol in a car,"
- During rainy or snowy days, please keep wet boots/shoes /umbrellas on the floor (not on the seat).
- Keep your language clean.. (Have soap and water on hand).
- Keep your hands inside the car and, don't yell (out the window) to other cars.
- If you know a shortcut, feel free to suggest this to the driver.
- Don't use the app as a game. In other words, don't schedule a ride and then cancel as soon as the driver arrives.
- Be sure to check the seat for personal belongings: keys, credit cards, phones, electronic vapers, etc., before you leave the car.

- If the driver offers you candy, don't take the whole bag.
- If your ride involves an added stop, please give the driver an estimate of the amount of time it's going to take at the stop.
- Don't expect your driver to speed to your destination.
- If you request a stop at a drive-up window, be polite. Keep your transaction courteous.
- Conditions which may cause you to .be refused:
  - Under 18 years old
  - No car seat for your child
  - Rude or crude behavior
  - An excess number of passengers
  - Smoking or drinking alcohol
  - Too drunk to stand up (especially with drivers who aren't willing to pick you up off the ground.)
  - Any indiscretion stated from the driver

ABOUT THE AUTHOR

I often ask my riders – "Are you living your dream?"

My response is, "Yes, I'm living my dream. My imagination took form as a youngster as I created roads between clumps of grass in the front yard and drove matchbox cars in and around the make-believe towns.

When I was in junior high, I wrote stories for children during study hall instead of doing homework. My parents encouraged my hobby by paying tuition to the Institute of Children's Literature for a correspondence writing course while I was in high school.

Thirty years complete with two marriages, three states, six children, numerous jobs, and eight grandchildren, kept me from my desire to write and publish a book..

By 2013, I lived in an empty nest. No husband, no children at home. Needing to survive, I came out of the closet . With my voice (through writing) I share a message of love and acceptance for all. My dream to be an author came true in 2015. Combining the love of travel and writing, led me to publish this book. I hope you enjoy it."

Susan W Shafer

Made in the USA
Coppell, TX
14 August 2021

60503520R00096